*Start Your Ou*

# DAY SPA

**Learner
Services**

AND MORE

Additional titles in *Entrepreneur's* **Startup Series**

## *Start Your Own*

Entrepreneur
MAGAZINE'S

# *startup*

## *Start Your Own*

# DAY SPA
# AND MORE

## *Destination Spa • Medical Spa*
## *Yoga Center • Spiritual Spa*

### *Entrepreneur Press and Preethi Burkholder*

Ep
Entrepreneur
Press

Editorial Director: Jere L. Calmes
Managing Editor: Marla Markman
Cover Design: Beth Hansen-Winter
Production and Composition: Eliot House Productions

This publication is designed to provide accurate and authoritative information in regard to the subject matter covered. It is sold with the understanding that the publisher is not engaged in rendering legal, accounting or other professional services. If legal advice or other expert assistance is required, the services of a competent professional person should be sought.

**Library of Congress Cataloging-in-Publication Data**

Burkholder, Preethi.
   Start your own day spa and more/by Entrepreneur Press and Preethi Burkholder.
      p.    cm.
   Includes index.
   ISBN-13: 978-1-59918-122-6 (alk. paper)
   ISBN-10: 1-59918-122-3 (alk. paper)
      1. Health resorts. 2. Entrepreneurship. I. Title.
RA794.B87 2007
613'.122—dc22                                        2007023239

Printed in Canada
12 11 10 09 08                                        10 9 8 7 6 5 4 3 2

# Contents

*Appendix*

# Preface

This book is about achieving your dreams. About doing what you love and having the money follow. Think how wonderful it would be to become financially and emotionally independent, work on your own terms, and do what you love for a living. Yes, you can have it all. By the time you finish reading (or in some cases browsing) this book, you will have acquired the technical, practical, and spiritual tools that you need to start your own spa and run a profitable business.

There lies an entrepreneurial spirit within each of us. At some level, most of us dream of achieving something to make our lives better. It may be a flickering flame or a dying ember, but it is there. This book serves as an incentive to spark that flame and make it into a bright light. This book will show you how to cultivate that entrepreneurial spirit and become a successful spa owner.

*Start Your Own Day Spa and More* is about integrating your hidden talents, the confidence you never knew you had, and your knowledge (perhaps new) of the spa industry. The motivation to start your own spa may be due to the loss of a job, a feeling of unfulfilment in your current job, not making enough money, being tired of taking orders from a dysfunctional boss, or hitting bottom in your emotional life.

Will every reader of this book start a spa business? Probably not. Maybe you don't want to become a spa owner just yet. It may be something you have thought about, but are not yet ready to put into action. This book plants fertile seeds within you so that by the time you are ready, you are armed with all the tools you need to execute your dream. Even if you don't become a lifelong entrepreneur in the spa industry, by learning how to start your own spa business you will develop an understanding of the business world that will make it much easier for you to get jobs and create a fulfilling work life for yourself.

This book is also intended to help you move beyond the theoretical aspects of running a business to embrace the practical business and creative matters that are vital to the day-to-day operations of a successful business. If you already own a spa business, the pages that unfold may be worth reviewing to help you improve or consider new options for running your current business.

The desire for money alone is not a strong enough reason to start a business. Any business, large or small, needs to make money to survive and grow. However, money cannot be the sole motivating factor for you to become a successful spa owner. You need to have passion, a burning desire for your dream to come true. No one can take this passion away from you—except you.

If you have doubts about your motivation, then this is probably not your time to take the plunge. If you don't feel that level of passion about your venture, then you should reevaluate your plans of becoming a spa owner. Let this book be the deciding force that ignites your passion to spark that dying flame or kindle it until you are certain about what you want to do.

*Start Your Own Day Spa and More* gives you the courage and impetus that you need to do what you love in the spa industry (and other industries, too). It is about discovering that inner potential within you to start your own business and do what you love in life. You need to have three key ingredients: a burning desire, willingness to work like it's nobody's business, and a spiritual plan. Combine all these with a positive attitude and you will be running a successful spa in no time.

My father once told me a story that has had a profound impact on my pursuing what I love and becoming successful at it. "Two men, out of prison, were free at last. One looked below and saw mud; the other looked up and saw the stars." My father turned to me and asked, "Which do you want to be—the one who points his face at the mud, or the one who aims for the stars?"

Today, I have hitched my wagon to a star. My father's philosophy has helped me to aim high in life. It taught me as a child and now as an adult, to believe in myself and to not settle for less. Always aim for the top and believe in yourself. Climb until your dreams come true.

*To My Dear Father in Heaven*

# 1

# Simply Spa

More and more people are embracing a more natural, holistic, and fulfilling lifestyle through spa living. They look for simple pleasures that spas offer. The motivation for people to go to spas has shifted from not only seeking relaxation and de-stressing but also to achieving and maintaining health and wellness.

# A Spa Lifestyle: Back to Basics

A working mother needs some quiet time for herself. A couple wants to revive their flawed marriage. A corporate CEO wants to rediscover spirituality. A bride-to-be wants a night of pampering with her friends. A teenager is troubled by acne. A baby boomer wants her wrinkles to disappear. A hospice patient needs some TLC in his dying moments. A pregnant woman wants to ease her back pain. An alcoholic decides to become sober.

Where can all these people go for comfort, pampering, and wellness? Spas. People seek spas for various reasons including

- Pampering and pleasure
- Stress management
- Health and wellness
- Fitness
- Weight loss
- Spiritual reconnection
- Anti-aging treatments
- Relaxation and entertainment

Spas offer a wide variety of services to meet diverse needs. Swedish massage, Japanese Shiatsu, Thai massage, electrolysis, European facials, acupuncture, Dead Sea salt scrubs, Moor mud wraps, thalassotherapy, aromatherapy, reflexology, haircutting, manicures, microdermabrasion, endermologie, Reiki, Botox, cellulite firming, weight loss, tanning, meditation, yoga, Tai Chi, tooth whitening, Ayurveda herbal bath, and state-of-the-art fitness programs with personal trainers are just a handful of treatments offered at spas, which have become popular places for healing.

The International Spa Association (ISPA) defines the "ten domains of Spa," or segments of the industry, as:

1. "The Waters"
2. Food, nourishment, diet, and nutrition
3. Movement, exercise, and fitness
4. Touch, massage, and bodywork
5. Mind/body/spirit
6. Aesthetics, skin care, natural beauty agents
7. Physical space, climatology, global ecology
8. Social/cultural arts and values, spa culture
9. Management, marketing, and operations

**Tip...**

## Smart Tip
With less time available for rest and regeneration, people are seeking places to revive themselves, to gain relief from overindulgence and overwork. Spas are the answer.

10. Time, rhythm, and cycles

The shape of spas is continually in a state of flux. Defining the kinds of spas in existence today can get a little tricky because of the variety of treatments offered. Consequently, categorizing spas is difficult.

For the sake of clarity, spas in this book have been loosely placed in four categories:

1. *Day spa*. A place to spend the day and get massages, facials, and body treatments, among other healing and beauty services. Clients don't spend the night in these facilities, hence the name. Examples of day spas include tanning salons, hair and nail salons, mobile spas, and spa parties.

2. *Destination spa*. A destination spa is one where clients come for relaxation, healing, and beauty treatments. These spas offer all-inclusive treatments ranging from yoga to weight-loss programs. Clients may spend anywhere from one day to a week (or even longer) at destination spas. Rates can be from $500 to $25,000 a week, or more. Examples of destination spas include resort spas, hotel spas, and cruise ship spas.

3. *Medical spa*. Here traditional hospital medicine and alternative therapies cross paths. Medical spas include dental spas, Botox treatment centers, wellness centers, and hospital-based medical centers.

4. *Spiritual spa*. A spiritual spa connects people on a spiritual level. Spiritual spas include eco holistic spas, meditation centers, Reiki healing centers, spa retreats, and yoga centers.

More and more people are returning to age-old tested treatments like Feng Shui, acupuncture, and music therapy for comfort and wellness. They are reconnecting with each other through the power of natural healing offered by spas. The spa life is back to basics, reconnecting with one's inner self and embracing a more natural, holistic, and fulfilling lifestyle. Today, a spa lifestyle has come to mean a yearning for the simple life, polished by current technological advancements.

Simply spa!

> **Tip...**
>
> **Smart Tip**
> The modern spa is descended from the ancient practice of bathing in hot springs and mineral waters.

# A Little Spa History

Spa-going and massage therapy are often described as new cultural trends, but in fact, they have been practiced for centuries. The practice of massage, which is a central part of spa living, dates back to the Chinese, who provide the earliest mention of massage in a book dating to about 2700 B.C.: "Early morning stroking with the palm of the hand, after the night's sleep, when the blood is rested and the tempers relaxed, protects against colds, keeps the organs supple and prevents minor ailments." Egyptian tomb paintings depict people being massaged. Some 3,000 to 5,000 years ago the Hindus developed Ayurveda, which means "the science of long life." As the traditional Indian system of medicine, it placed great emphasis on the therapeutic benefits of massage with aromatic oils, herbs, and spices. Hippocrates, considered the father of modern medicine, spoke of massage in the 4th century B.C.: "A physician must be experienced in many things," he wrote, "but assuredly in rubbing, for rubbing can bind a joint that is too loose, and loosen a joint that is too rigid."

# Cleansing Waters

Water has always been seen as a cleansing and healing agent. The word *spa* is from the Latin *salus per aquam*, which means "health from water." *Spa* is also the name of a small village in Belgium where hot mineral springs were discovered by the ancient Romans and used by their soldiers to treat the aching muscles and wounds from battle. According to Chinese Feng Shui, when the water element is balanced, happiness prevails in one's life's journey and one has the ability to go with the flow. When it is not in balance one experiences dissatisfaction and has a tendency to hold on to things. In the Christian religion the Baptism ceremony uses water to cleanse the believer. Early spa use was largely male. Today however, more women frequent spas.

Social bathing was an important cultural process practiced by Mesopotamians, Egyptians, Minoans, Greeks, Chinese, Indians, and Romans whenever they sought health and relief from pain and diseases. Homer and other Greek writers indicated that as early as 500 B.C. the Greeks favored a variety of baths, from hot water tubs to hot-air baths, or laconica. From the small Greek laconica grew the Roman *balneum* and finally the extravagant Roman *thermae*, from the Greek word for "heat." Thermae also means a large-scale spa. Emperor Agrippa designed and created the first thermae in 25 B.C. The thermae later became a central entertainment complex offering sports, restaurants, and various types of baths, the equivalent of a modern day, luxurious destination spa. Although Romans were not the first ancient civilization to indulge in social bathing, they were definitely the civilization that perfected it.

It is not known when the Romans used the first public bath, but during the reign of Augustus Caesar from 27 B.C. to 14 A.D., there were approximately 170 baths throughout Rome. By 43 A.D., the Roman public had taken on a different view of baths and bathing. It began to view baths as a way of providing rest and relaxation to all people, not just those weary of war.

With the fall of the Roman Empire came the demise of the Roman bath. But over the centuries, baths and spas eventually spread throughout Europe, becoming increasingly elaborate. Across the ocean, in the still undiscovered "New World," native cultures were enjoying the benefits of hot spring therapy. Native Americans bathed in mineral springs to enhance their physical and spiritual health, and these baths played an important role in the social structure of their communities.

In 737 A.D., Japan's first *onsen*, or hot spring, opened. Saunas began appearing along the Baltic in Finland as early as 1000 A.D., inaugurating a rich Finnish spa-going tradition. The Ottomans were famous for their *hammam* (public bathhouse), the crowning example being the Baths of Roxelana built in 1556.

By the dawn of the 20th century, spas began to be molded into a different shape. Scientific clinics and public hospitals replaced the spa environs, and existing spas eventually turned into vacation lodges. The original association of spas with water faded.

The modern day spa is an interesting combination of ancient traditions and modern technological wonders. Today, the value of prevention, anti-aging treatments, healthy lifestyles, alternative medicine, and relaxation have been rediscovered and appreciated anew. Yet, the essence of the modern spa remains the same as its roots. It is about healing.

# Researching the
## Spa Market

This is a great time to get into the spa business. The number of consumers is growing; they have the money to spend, and they are willing to spend it in spas. The day spa industry by itself is a $12.4 billion industry. Spas have taken off like wildfire. Just in the last decade, the popularity of aesthetic and health spa services has soared, transforming this industry into a multi-billion dollar business. Spas have altered the way people think about health, beauty, and happiness. The spa business is one of *the* service-oriented businesses to be in right now.

Several reasons have brought on the tremendous explosion in the number of spas.

- The hectic pace of work and many lifestyles have put enormous stress on people and created a need for a healthy outlet. Spas are seen as great stress relievers. Stress, in fact, is the number-one reason people seek spa treatments.

**Stat Fact**
According to the International Spa Association (ISPA), the number of spas in the U.S. grew at an annual rate of 21 percent from 1995 to 1999 and aggregate industry revenues grew by 114 percent between 2000 and 2002.

- People seek to change their direction or behavior. They want to lose weight, become spiritually fit, and enjoy beauty treatments. Spas offer these changes of direction.

- A spa experience is a continuous process that can be integrated into one's daily life once people return home from a spa vacation.

- Consumers are becoming more aware of how spas offer alternative methods of treating minor aches and pains. Pills cannot fix all of life's ailments.

- Modern technology, fast foods, digital music, automobiles, and computers have transformed the pace in our lives, so instant gratification has become the norm. People live disconnected from each other in their work, home, and social environments. The spa lifestyle helps to slow down this pace and create a yearning for the simple, communal life, where connecting with one another is key.

The increasing interest in skin has also impacted spa growth. Skin care has evolved throughout the decades and has become a necessity in American culture, as well as a specialized market within the general scope of cosmetology. What really has placed skin care on the map, however, is Americans' fascination with noninvasive, anti-aging treatments. Statistics from the American Society for Aesthetic Plastic Surgery indicate that this demand has increased more than 450 percent in the last four years. Once considered a niche market, anti-aging skin care has now become the cornerstone around which most spas are built. Furthermore, anti-aging products no longer target just older people. Teens, women in their 20s, and working men in their 30s are more educated about taking care of their skin on a long-term basis and start anti-aging treatments at an early age.

**Stat Fact**
Over 47 percent of the spa goers visit these places of "pampering" to relieve stress, according to the International Spa Association Statistics, 2006.

The economic potential in anti-aging treatments is exploding at an unimaginable rate. According to a 2006 study by Packaged Facts, a leading consumer goods research firm, the U.S. market for anti-aging products is estimated at $12.4 billion and has the potential to expand to more than $16 billion by 2010, with skin care products and treatments controlling 52 percent of retail sales. Increasingly, consumers are opening their wallets to purchase anti-aging products and professional anti-aging treatments.

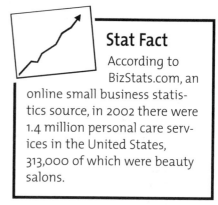

**Stat Fact**
According to BizStats.com, an online small business statistics source, in 2002 there were 1.4 million personal care services in the United States, 313,000 of which were beauty salons.

With all these statistics indicating a booming future for the spa industry, why not seize the opportunity and start your own spa? Carpe diem. Strike while the iron is hot!

# Finding Your Niche

Finding your niche means being something to someone and not everything to everybody. In other words, it refers to owning a space in your customer's mind. "Spa niche" raises the following question: "Who is your target market?" Identifying your spa niche will be a critical component for the success of your business. Spas must define their role within the marketplace, develop a clear identity, and fulfill a particular need.

A spa business does not grow by accident. Rather, growth must be pursued as an actual business objective. Comprehending what your immediate business opportunities, strengths, and weaknesses are and understanding the demographics of the clientele in your area can affect the way that you present your business to them, and ultimately how you are perceived by this market.

Categorizing people is not something that can be done in the spa business. There is no typical spa-goer. As spas have become more and more commonplace, the services that they provide have shifted from an unnecessary extravagance to an essential part of balanced self-care for many. Spas have been typically associated with the aristocrats, the elite, and the wealthy. Not anymore. The wealthy no longer have exclusive use of spas. Spas are now accessible to a much broader population. The billionaire's wife and the construction worker alike can de-stress at the same spa for the same price and quality of service.

**Stat Fact**
According to Leading Spas of Canada (www.leadingspasof canada.org), there was a 153 percent increase in spa visits in Canada between 2001 and 2003.

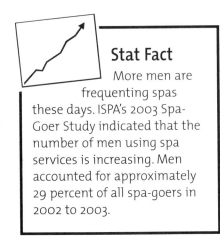

**Stat Fact**

More men are frequenting spas these days. ISPA's 2003 Spa-Goer Study indicated that the number of men using spa services is increasing. Men accounted for approximately 29 percent of all spa-goers in 2002 to 2003.

The average age of the spa visitor is changing. The beginning of the 1990s saw spa clients in their late 30s to early 50s; the age of today's spa user is younger, and ranges from the early 20s to the mid-60s.

Spas are increasingly being used as corporate meeting grounds for movers and shakers. They are helping to promote professional work environments and philanthropic activities within companies. For example, some banks offer free massage treatments to their employees once a week. This helps to create a healthy workforce, connect employees with one another, and create a happy work environment.

As a spa owner, it is your responsibility to know exactly who buys what you are selling and then clearly focus your marketing efforts on those individuals. If the target market is not properly identified, your spa can find itself hopelessly cornered, trying to be all things to all people. You don't want to be hunting needles in haystacks when it comes to seeking customers. Pinpoint your message and pick out your prospects carefully. Know your customer population.

There are wide ranges of customer requirements, perceptions, and expectations for any service in the marketplace. Unless a spa custom produces its services for each customer, it must optimize its efforts for maximum gain.

There will come a point where you are compelled to say, "Enough with the applause, now show me the money." In other words, you will soon tire of listening to compliments about your services from a loosely defined target market that is not producing revenue. Those who are not within your target market will not buy, regardless of what you say or have to offer. They will have unlimited compliments but will not spend money on your services. To this end, it is imperative that you do not waste your precious dollars making general statements that get attention but don't sell the goods.

As a spa owner, you must be able to predict market behavior using the laws of supply and demand. This will help you make good business decisions. If you believe that the demand for a product or service is going to rise, for instance, start selling that product because the price that people are willing to pay for it is going to rise, too. For example, there is likely to be more demand for bikini waxes, body wraps, and body scrubs during the summer than in the winter because more men and women wear shorts, swimsuits, and other clothes that expose their bodies during the summer. So, plan accordingly. Offer

**Tip...**

**Smart Tip**

Spa trends include male-friendly spas, teen spas, hospice spas, corporate spa programs, and family spas.

## Understanding Your Clientele Worksheet

Estimated number of clients _____

Average age of client _____

Average income _____

Employment status _____

Education level _____

Product/service that is most popular _____

Number of women _____

Number of men _____

Number of teenagers _____

Average yearly/monthly expenditure on spa services _____

these services during the summertime. Use the worksheet above to better understand your clientele.

# Competitors: Rivals or Collaborators?

Understanding and acknowledging your competition is an important strategic tool that will help you grow and develop a unique selling proposition. Denying your competition could be the biggest mistake you make as a spa owner. Critically assess your competition. For some spa owners, investigating other spa businesses might feel too much like spying. If you fall into this category, have someone that you trust do the spying for you, but don't overlook this critical factor of assessing your competitors.

Some spa owners dread other businesses as rivals. Viewing your competitors as collaborators can actually be more profitable and emotionally healthy both for you as an individual and for your business, too. Competition brings out the best in you because it makes you strive harder to succeed. Competition is a good thing.

The first step is to identify your competition. Open the telephone book and scan the Yellow Pages or the business directory. See what complementary businesses are in your area. For example, retail stores providing beauty and skin care products and a

**Beware!**
Understanding and acknowledging your competition is an important strategic tool. Denying your competition is a big mistake.

laundry service that cleans spa linens are also your competitors. Introduce yourself to massage therapists, estheticians, Reiki practitioners, yoga masters, fitness trainers, physical therapists, skin and body workers, chiropractors, acupuncturists, and physicians in your area. The more people who know you as a spa professional, the more opportunity there is for them to assist you in your professional growth. Knowing a large number of health professionals gives you a broad perspective in your area of expertise. Be as involved in the total spa picture as you can. Network; don't isolate.

Having a solid understanding of the competitors in your market helps you better understand your own business and its place in the competitive environment. Once you have determined who your competition is, it is time to evaluate what is working for and against them. Start a file on each of your major competitors. Gather as much of their marketing, promotional, and sales material as possible. What kinds of images are your competitors portraying? If you were a potential customer, what would attract you to their businesses? What type of customers are they trying to appeal to? Is it exactly the same market as you are targeting, or are they appealing to a customer base you have overlooked? Do they have products and services that you don't offer your spa customers? Where are their businesses weak? How can you supply a service to make up for that deficiency? How vulnerable are your competitors to changing market conditions? Where do you measure? Ask yourself as many analytical questions as you can.

Assessing your competition must become an integral part of your ongoing analysis of your own operations as well as the entire operating environment. Competitive intelligence will tell you what services you should be offering, how you can present them to existing and potential customers, and how to improve your position in your industry relative to your competitors.

Competitive intelligence is something that every smart spa owner needs to do on a continual basis. It is not a one-time thing. Rather, competition is the process of uncovering, analyzing, and presenting publicly available information on your business's competitors in order to maintain a competitive edge in the marketplace. Use the Competitive Analysis Worksheet on page 13 to analyse your competition.

Competitive intelligence helps you to analyze the following:

- Are there networking opportunities that you should be pursuing that your competitors have missed?
- Are there other spa products and services you should be offering your customers?
- Should you offer higher quality services and products?
- How can you improve your customer service in order to make your spa customers more loyal to your establishment?

## Competitive Analysis Worksheet

Business name: _____

Address: _____

Contacts: _____

Years in Business: _____

Products and Services: _____

Pricing Structure: _____

**SWOT Analysis**

**S**trengths: _____

**W**eaknesses: _____

**O**pportunities: _____

**T**hreats: _____

Other Notes: _____

_____

- Are there other customer groups that you should be targeting? Maybe teens, men, kids, and pregnant women?
- How can you position yourself to be better able to capitalize on opportunities and weather threats?
- What can you do to improve your marketing, promotional, and sales materials?
- Can you pursue more free media attention to promote your spa?
- Should you be accepting additional forms of payment to make it easier for your customers to pay? For example, instead of only accepting cash and checks, maybe introduce Paypal, credit cards, and in-house accounts.

# Starting from Scratch: Planning a Spa

Opening a spa is a big step. It requires confidence in your professional skills, your business ability, and your commitment to your vocation. Examine the pros and cons of starting your own spa before taking the plunge. Perhaps it is still an infant dream for some of you, a dream that will silently swell as the years unfold. Others may be ready to finally take that bold step of starting their own spa.

In order to start and run a successful spa business, you need to have skills in business building, business management, and a basic understanding of what spas are about. Some people who have become successful spa owners had no clue of what any of these were when they started out. Instead, they were "spa savvy" and hired the right team of people to do the work for them. Others learned along the way and succeeded at running a profitable spa business. These are the self learners. You are getting a head start by reading this book because it teaches you what you need to know about starting and running a successful spa operation.

The fundamental aspiration of every spa operation, whether it be day, destination, medical, or spiritual spa, is to become a strong and healthy business. Spas cater to different lifestyles and needs, mostly focusing on pampering the customer. Understanding consumer needs can affect the way a spa business performs. The best spa operations are those that advocate sincerity and authenticity throughout the entire fabric of their service.

Each spa owner may have cultivated his/her own ideas for building a spa business. Consequently, there are no set guidelines on starting a spa. However, here are some useful suggestions.

# Get a Good Footing

The first question to ask is, "What kind of spa do you want to open?" Spas are service-oriented businesses. So, build your planning around the type of spa you want to open. This is a good time to flesh out the basics of planning. The planning phase of opening a spa is critical and time consuming. Get a good footing by planning the type of spa you want to open.

# Location, Location, Location

Where you will build your spa is another consideration. Location can be an important factor in establishing the profitability of your business. Selecting the right location is key. Some may select to run a home spa, while others will prefer an established location with demographics that suit the clientele you are seeking. Decide whether you want to build your own spa from scratch or to buy an existing business.

# Selecting a Theme

A theme that reflects the spa's environment, logo, and design can help with name recognition and ultimately build a strong brand for your business. Once a theme has been selected, you can build the furniture, lighting, food, linen, décor, and music around it. For example, if it is an Ayurveda theme that you have selected, then playing Indian ragas in the background and the creation of a small Buddha garden in the outdoor space will complement your spa environment.

## Spas for Men and Women

Although the majority of spa-goers are women, more men are frequenting spas nowadays. Plan your theme to address the tastes of both men and women. This will help to draw clients of both sexes and increase your profit margins. Fluffy pillows, ribbons, and lace can yield a rather feminine look, making some men feel unwelcome. Balance your décor with photos of male spa treatments, dark colored couches, and a menu card that provides services to men.

## Marketing Efforts

Chapter 8 gives some great marketing ideas for spa owners. Depending on how high you may want to go, the tips given in that chapter can cost you less than $100 each. Embark on a continuous marketing campaign and diversify your marketing strategies. Don't put all your eggs in one basket.

# Start-Up
# Funding

The most crucial part of starting a spa is having enough cash flow to get through the start-up phase. Proper planning of the business is also necessary to ensure that the fledgling spa gets off to a good start. Some ways to get start-up funding are discussed in this chapter.

# Debt Financing

Debt is a common source for funding new businesses. Debt financing can take many forms, but it basically means that a lender has loaned you funds that you are obligated to repay in the future. Debt financing does not involve an ownership stake in the business but simply a promise to pay. Once you have determined the dollar amount of capital that you need to fund the start-up phase of your spa, it is time to start evaluating the potential sources of financing. Remember, it may be difficult for you to attract outside capital before you have established a track record.

## Your Own Resources: Money from Personal Savings, Family, and Friends

This is the first place you should start—for many reasons. First, using your own funds is the least risky proposition from an asset seizure point of view. You (the lender or investor) are not likely to foreclose on you (the borrower). Second, external lenders want to see that you have funds at risk.

Other financing may be scarce in the beginning, and the more of your own savings you have, the greater the likelihood of financial stability and growth. You may have to save for a considerable amount of time to start your own business. It is important to remember, however, that just as you wouldn't invest all of your life's savings in a single stock, you shouldn't put all of your eggs in the same basket by dumping all of your savings into your business. Make sure that you have a number of saving vehicles for the future.

Proceed with caution when borrowing start-up funding from friends, relatives, and in-laws. Some may genuinely want to help you out by giving you that little boost when you are first starting out. Others may be shrewd investors, wanting to make money off you at a vulnerable stage in your life, knowing that you will walk barefoot over broken glass to pay them back. Sometimes they may have savings in the bank but will give you a loan at a higher interest than the bank, knowing that you have been denied by a finance institution. So, beware!

## Bank Loans

The bank is the most common source of lending for small businesses. Most businesses don't need a tremendous amount of outside financing to start or sustain the venture. In fact, many begin with less than $10,000 in working capital. However, many conventional bank loans are not well suited for micro loans (under $10,000) or to finance new businesses. If you have already tried your bank with little success, don't despair. There are a number of special loan programs available for even the smallest businesses. Some are designed for loans of up to $100,000 or more, while others can address the micro-loan needs that often arise in a massage business.

Bankers are likely to ask these questions when you apply for a loan:

1. *How much money do you want?* There are two schools of thought on this issue. One says to obtain the largest loan you can possibly get; the other says to go for the minimal loan that will get you through the first six to nine months of operation while you build your relationship and track record with the banker. It is easier to get the second type. The banking institution can come in six to nine months later with an additional loan to support a growing spa business.

2. *What are you going to do with the money?* Be specific in identifying how the loan will be used.

3. *What are the benefits to your company?* What does borrowing additional funds and taking the additional risk do for the company?

4. *When will the loan be repaid?* The key factor is the source of repayment. If it is going to come within a short time, such as within one year, then it can be a single payment loan. If it is going to require payment from cash flow, it should be a term loan spread out over several years.

5. *How is the loan going to be repaid?* It could be any of the following: (1) cash flow, which would repay a long-term capital loan; (2) turnover of inventory and receivables and a leveling off of inventory; or (3) refinancing from another financing source.

6. *What are your contingency plans?* What if something happens so the loan cannot be repaid on schedule? You need to spell out what is it going to take to generate the funds necessary to repay the bank loan.

Here are some questions for you to ask the banker:

- *What are the banker's (or bank's) experiences and feelings about businesses in the spa industry?* Is it something they have had good or bad loan experience with? Or is this one area where they haven't had any experience at all?

- *How long has the loan officer been with the bank?*

## Bright Idea

A bank loan is a great way to get funding to start your spa. It is vital to communicate with your banker before signing on a loan. After all, banks don't give loans; bankers do.

- *What is the bank's "CAMEL" rating?* This is an acronym for a system that has been used by federal and state regulatory agencies in recent years to rate the bank's performance. It covers five separate categories: capital, assets, management, earnings, liquidity (CAMEL). These five separate categories are rated from 1 to 5, 1 being excellent, 5 representing a serious problem.
- *What additional information will the bank need beyond your business plan?* Does it want projections for three to five years or does it want to see an accounts receivable aging?
- *What is the turnaround time on loans?* Once these items are submitted, when do you get a decision?

## Small Business Administration

The Small Business Administration (SBA) is a government agency set up to help small businesses succeed. A small business loan can be the tool that nets you enough capital to create your dreams. Not only is this organization a great resource for finding capital, but it can also provide the small business owner with invaluable advice on getting started and seeking loans from other sources.

Some of the loan programs offered through the Small Business Loan Administration include:

- SBA low-documentation loans
- SBA micro-loans
- Other micro-loan programs

## Leasing Companies

Leasing companies specialize in financing manufacturing or office equipment. You may find that the company that you purchase the equipment from has its own leasing arm and can handle the entire transaction for you. Equipment leases are always secured by the equipment that is being leased. If you fall behind on your payments, you risk losing the equipment. On the other hand, the interest rates tend to be low because of its secured nature and also because the leasing company may be using the lease as a purchase incentive.

# Winning a Grant to Help Start Your Spa

Learning how to write winning grant proposals is an invaluable asset for spa owners. The world of grants opens opportunities for massage therapists, medical professionals, beauty practitioners, healers, body workers, and skin care professionals to get free money for spa-related education, research, and business opportunities.

Grant seeking is not a special talent that one has to be born with; rather, it is a skill that can be developed over time. Writing proposals costs time, not money. Winning a grant is more than a financial experience. It enriches your esteem, confidence, and inner soul. Unlike debt financing, grants don't have to be repaid. They are yours to spend.

# Grant Proposal Elements

The connection between applicants and potential funders is the grant proposal. You may think that writing a grant proposal is a daunting task, something that is extremely difficult and time consuming. Not really. What distinguishes one proposal from another is thoughtful, systematic, cohesive writing.

Addressing the following five questions can help you to develop your project idea into a feasible plan. Their answers are the main elements of a grant proposal.

1. What is the community need that the plan is addressing?

   Answering this question develops the *need statement* of a proposal.

2. What would an improved community situation look like?

   Answering this question develops the *goals and objectives* components of a proposal.

3. What can you do to improve the situation?

   Answering this question develops the *methodology* component of a proposal.

4. How will you determine the project success/failure?

   Answering this question develops the *evaluation* component of a proposal.

5. How much will the project cost?

   Answering this question develops the *budget* component of a proposal.

By focussing on causes, future spa owners can seek funding for the following (and many more):

- Opening a spa
- Paying for college to attend massage therapy school
- Payment for massage classes/certification
- Travel grants to attend trade shows and spa conferences
- Purchasing spa equipment
- Traveling overseas to study spa treatments

The internet has numerous web sites that offer information on where to find grants for small business start-ups. Here are some of them:

- *www.fdncenter.org.* This is the Foundation Center web site. It offers information about funders, donors, seminars, and award information, among other things.

Click on "Funding Sources" and move to "Grantmaker web sites." There are three categories under grantmaker web site: private foundations, community foundations, and corporations. "Private Foundations" are recommended for the beginner level grant seeker.

- *www.grants.gov*. This web site provides organizations with information necessary to search for federal government grants. Click on "Find Grant Opportunities." Under "Select grant opportunities," do a basic search by typing in your field of interest. You will get a listing of funding available under each field. This site gives the funding agency, the sub agency, funding opportunity number, CFDA number, program name, and closing date. It keeps applicants informed of the newest grants under a section titled "Grants Made Available in the Last 7 Days."

- *www.cof.org*. This is the Council on Foundations web site. It provides information on foundations awarding grants, upcoming events such as grants conferences and career programs, how to start a foundation, grant making activities, publications, or you can type a question such as "How do I get a Grant?" www.cof.org details emerging issues in philanthropy. It gives accurate definitions of private operating foundations, and public foundations.

Don't forget that part of your grant writing will include a business plan. See Chapter 5 for more information on what needs to be in your business plan.

# 4

# Confessions
# of an
# Entrepreneur

The world of business consists of two groups: the creative and the practical. These two groups view the world from very different perspectives. The creative people have an instinctive, gut-level appreciation for presentation, uniqueness, and delivery of service. The practical people on the other hand have an instinctive, gut-level appreciation for numbers and analysis. Within the creative and practical groups, there are leaders and followers. Take it from Tuco in the movie *The Good, the Bad, and the Ugly* who says, "There are two types of people in this world, my friend. Those with the gun and those who dig." Those with the gun set the overall direction, and those who dig sweat and do the work. An entrepreneur is a leader who is able to balance the creative and practical elements and create a following to sell a product or service.

In an ideal world, you would have to have a blend of both worlds in order to start your own spa successfully, but this rarely happens. Most people are lopsided but continue to be successful entrepreneurs. They make up for their deficits by hiring professionals, seeking advice from others, and self-study.

It doesn't matter whether you are creative or practical, a leader or a follower. You can become a successful entrepreneur if you have motivation, a willingness to learn, and a positive spirit. It's cultivating your entrepreneurial spirit that is vital to your success as a spa owner. See Traits of an Entrepreneur on page 25 to see which you have and which you need to work on or get help with.

# Why Do You Want to Open a Spa?

Although at its core entrepreneurship is about selling, the desire for money alone is not a strong enough reason to start a business. Any business, large or small, needs to make money to survive and grow. However, money cannot be the sole, motivating factor if you want your business to become a success. As the owner, you need to have passion and a burning desire for your dream to come true. If you don't feel that level of passion about your venture, then you should reevaluate your plans of becoming a spa owner. You can think about it, but avoid taking the initiative to start a spa until you have the passion.

Ask yourself why you want to open a spa. Is it because you are passionate about wellness and want to help people rediscover balance? In addition, envisioning healthy profit margins could also be a motivating factor. Perhaps it is a mixture of both. Optimum results tend to flow from a combination of sincere belief in the good you wish to impart to people and the requirement of sustainable fiscal profitability arising from your business initiative.

# Are You an Entrepreneur?

Starting your own spa requires an entrepreneurial spirit, a spirit that is within each of us. For some, that spirit may be weak at the moment, while in others it may be an enduring passion. Some factors can determine whether you have what it takes to become an entrepreneur right now.

# Traits of an Entrepreneur

○ *The power of a positive attitude.* No matter how many entrepreneurial characteristics you have or develop, they won't do any good unless you combine them with a positive attitude. Entrepreneurs are optimists. They have to be in order to see opportunities where others see only problems.

○ *Vision.* The ability to see the end results of your goals while working to achieve them.

○ *Confidence.* The belief that you can do what you set out to do.

○ *Perseverance.* The refusal to quit; the willingness to keep goals in sight and work toward them, despite obstacles.

○ *Drive.* The desire to work hard to accomplish your goals, not giving up.

○ *Honesty.* The commitment to tell the truth and deal with people fairly.

○ *Discipline.* The ability to stay focused and stick to schedules and deadlines.

○ *Adaptability.* The ability to cope with new situations and find creative solutions to problems.

○ *Competitiveness.* The willingness to compete with others.

○ *Organization.* The ability to structure your life and keep tasks and information in order.

○ *Persuasiveness.* The knack for convincing people to see your point of view and get them interested in your ideas; the ability to persuade another to buy your product or service.

○ *Risk taking.* The courage to expose yourself to possible losses; the ability to tread unknown waters.

○ *Understanding.* The ability to listen and empathize with other people.

○ *Dream.* The drive to achieve a dream that others thought was impossible.

○ *Effective time management.* The ability to manage time wisely and efficiently.

○ *Stress management.* The skills to manage stress well.

○ *Hard worker.* The presence of a strong work ethic.

○ *Motivation.* The ability to motivate others and your self.

○ *Comfortable with change.* The flexibility to go with the flow of things and be willing to change.

○ *Resilience.* The ability to recover from dire times and not give up.

Entrepreneurs see opportunities where others see problems. This trait is probably the fundamental one that distinguishes an entrepreneur from one who is not. Entrepreneurs have dreams and visions. They have the ability to move forward in spite of obstacles.

▲

Entrepreneurship is about freedom—the freedom to work how you want and when you want, the freedom to create your life from scratch and make it truly enjoyable and rewarding, and the freedom to do what you love. As an entrepreneur, you create your own schedule, one that meets your client's needs; you create your own opportunities; and you create a work environment that reflects your values, not those of someone else.

Entrepreneurship is not limited by your abilities or education. Rather, it is propelled by determination, persistence, and a stoic resilience in the face of rejection. You can develop your own unique market knowledge by applying your creativity and intelligence to your market.

To be an entrepreneur, you don't have to come up with a new invention or product. It is, however, necessary to provide a product or service that fills a consumer need. Entrepreneurship is about connecting your business ideas to the needs of your market. Entrepreneurs are constantly discovering new markets and trying to figure out how to supply those markets efficiently and at a profit.

---

# The Pros and Cons of Being an Entrepreneur

## Pros

○ *Independence*. When you own your own business, you do not have to follow orders or observe working hours set by someone else.

○ *Satisfaction*. Turning personal skills, hobbies, or other interests into your own business can be very satisfying.

○ *Financial reward*. Through hard work, the sky can be the limit. Countless small businesses have grown into large companies that have produced fortunes for their owners.

○ *Self-esteem*. Knowing you created something valuable can give you a strong sense of accomplishment, thus heightening your self-esteem.

## Cons

○ *Business failure*. Many small businesses fail. You risk not only losing your money but also the money invested in your business by others.

○ *Obstacles*. You will run into problems that you will have to solve by yourself. You may face discouragement from family and friends.

○ *Loneliness*. It can be lonely and even a little scary to be completely responsible for the success or failure of your business.

○ *Financial insecurity*. You are not guaranteed a set salary or any benefits.

○ *Long hours/hard work*. You will have to work long hours to get your business off the ground.

---

If you are a person who intensely dislikes change, you may want to seek a mental twist and tweak your die-hard thinking a little. After all, entrepreneurs need to be able to adapt and change according to the needs of consumers and the changing economy. Your spa business is never going to be static.

Setting deadlines for your goals is critical. Aim for tomorrow's goals today. Deadlines and time commitments drive action and make you move forward. Keep one eye on the long-term opportunity while taking care of today. Teach yourself to focus on the important things and to allow the less critical things to take a back seat.

You can also hand off tasks to a person who can take care of them for you. If you are a creative person and are not very good with numbers, then hire someone to do the accounting and taxes. Prioritize the most important tasks to help ensure that you spend time on those activities that make a difference. You will then move closer to achieving your goals.

Establish your business goals. If you could imagine the ideal spa setting, what would that be? Would it be a small, medium, or large facility? Would you like to own a tanning salon or a dental spa? What kinds of treatments will it perform? Will your spa be geared toward health or beauty practices?

When setting personal goals, be as specific as possible. Don't say that you want to earn "a decent and comfortable living." State that you plan to take home $4,000 a month during your first year of operation. The more specific you are, the easier it is to design a plan to reach those goals. Start with a goal you feel is realistic and work backwards, developing smaller goals along the way that will help you hit your target. Set goals that you can tackle.

Some goals that you may set for yourself may involve:

- How much money your spa will make each year
- How much money you will earn as the owner
- How many hours you will work each week
- The number of customers you will do business with during the first year
- How fast your spa will grow
- What ideas you have for expansion—locally, nationally, internationally
- The number of employees you will have on staff

Make writing your goals down a top priority. Keep in mind that committing your goals to paper will actually help you reach them. Once your targets are on paper, you can refer to them regularly to track your progress, change them as your spa's situation changes, and use them to keep everyone on your staff focused on what is truly important for your success as a business.

Starting and running a spa involves continuous learning. A lot of learning occurs from mistakes that you make along the way and vow never to repeat. Other learning comes from interactions you have with customers, fellow business owners, and friends who lead you towards success. Have the humility to accept advice. The faster you can adapt and adopt, the quicker your business will meet its goals. Make all the mistakes that you can while you still have your day job, before you venture out on your own.

# Tips for
# Starting a Spa

A successful spa is a combination of the technical, practical, and spiritual aspects that constitute a humming business. Here are some valuable tips that will help you to start and run a successful spa.

# Names that Sell

Creating a great business name is one of the best investments you will ever make. Your business name creates a million first impressions. The name of your spa represents the character of the enterprise to customers, investors, and the public. The best name is one that tells customers what your spa does. For example, Betty's Golden Tanning conveys the nature of the business better than Betty's Sunshine Corner. Choose your name wisely.

Your spa name and logo are closely connected. A logo should stay with you through the life of the business. When choosing a logo design, look at it in black-and-white, two- and four-color, and in both small and large versions. If necessary, hire a graphic designer to create a logo for your spa. It is worth the investment.

Another important factor to consider when choosing a name is the internet URL availability for that particular name. Make sure that the name you select leads to your business. Your web address needs to be the same or very similar to your business name. This makes it easier for your spa clients to find you.

Here are some things to think about when selecting a spa name:

- It must communicate essential information.
- It must be clear what your business is about. Many business names convey no clue as to what they do. Fountain Day Spa conveys what it does more than The Fountain.
- It must be easy to remember.
- It must avoid too exotic names or those that are hard to remember. Odd names can cost you customers.
- It must be legally available.
- It must not be in use already. If someone else has established prior rights to the name you wish to adopt, you will have to seek another one. Then remember to take the legal steps to protect your rights for the name you use.
- It must be easy to read, pronounce, and spell. If a stranger hearing or seeing your spa name for the first time has difficulty reading it, reconsider your decision. If potential customers draw a momentary blank, hesitate, and skip over it because it is difficult to pronounce, you should reconsider your choice.

## Dollar Stretcher

You can save money by doing a no-cost name search. Check the trademarks registered nationally on the U.S. Patent and Trademark Office web site www.uspto.gov.

## Testing your Spa Name

Test your spa name before you establish it. It is better to find out its marketability before registering it than after. Some simple, informal methods you can use to test your name are:

○ *Say your name aloud a number of times.* Listen to others say it. How does it sound, orally and visually?

○ *Talk to a few people and tell them the name that you want to use.* Gauge their responses.

○ *Conduct an informal opinion survey.* Keep your questions simple and be a good listener.

○ *Do a mail survey.* Mail a questionnaire to individuals or offices. Include a self-addressed stamped envelope

○ *Anticipate shortened versions of your name.* Can someone shorten it into something derogatory?

○ *Ask questions like:* "What does this name tell you?" "Do you like this name for a spa?" "Which one of these four names would work the best for a destination spa?"

• It must project the appropriate image to the intended audience. For example, if you name your spa "Winter Spa," it might create a seasonal image. Clients might wonder if you are open in the summertime.

• Your spa name must identify your "look-up" word. What is the most universal word describing the service that you render? Under what listing would someone look in the Yellow Pages? This is the look-up word.

# DBA

The Doing Business As (dba) filing is sometimes called a *fictitious name statement.* Filing the dba gives you the rights to the name within the jurisdiction of the governing body, which is typically your county. If you want to call your massage therapy services *Solar Mobile Massages*, you must file a form with the local authorities. This is usually done at the county clerk's office in the area where you plan to do business.

# Business Structures

The type of organization you create has a tremendous impact on profits and liability. Therefore you should make decisions about your legal form of operation early. In general, small businesses usually operate under three basic organizational structures: sole proprietorships, partnerships, and corporations. Each has its own advantages and disadvantages. A careful study of each type is recommended.

## Sole Proprietorship

Let's say you started to give stone therapies to people with aches and pains and got money in return. Well, guess what, you just became the head of a sole proprietorship. Once you begin providing services with the intention of making money, you become a sole proprietor of a business. Your business expenses are deductible, all income is taxable, and you assume the liabilities of the business. When you are the only one in charge of your business, you are the sole proprietor. You and your business are one.

A sole proprietorship is the most common and easiest type of business to create. Anyone who performs services of any kind, such as a manicurist, Ayurveda practitioner, Reiki healer, or spa interior designer is by default a sole proprietor, unless the business has been set up otherwise. A small company with only one employee is often kept as a sole proprietorship, but there are no restrictions on how big a sole proprietorship can become. It depends on the owner or proprietor.

In a sole proprietorship, all profits go directly to the owner. The disadvantage is that all legal and financial obligations incurred by the company are also passed directly to the owner. In a sole proprietorship, you are personally responsible for all of the business's obligations, such as debt and financing.

## Partnership

A partnership is formed whenever two or more people decide to enter a for-profit business venture. Typically each partner owns a portion of the company's profits and debts, which can be set up in a written agreement between the two parties. You do not need to file any special paperwork to form a partnership, but you should make sure you and your partner sign an agreement to minimize misunderstandings regarding each person's rights and liabilities.

When two or more people form a partnership, they are essentially married from a business standpoint. All liability is passed to the partners. There are two kinds of partnerships—limited and general. A limited partnership provides certain partners with a maximum financial liability equal to their investment. To maintain this limited financial liability status, these partners cannot participate in the daily operation of the business. The general partner is responsible for the day-to-day management of the business. Limited partners invest in the company and rely on the general partner to run the business.

## Corporation

A corporation is a separate legal entity created through the state where the business is incorporated. A corporation has owners who purchase shares in the corporation. The percentage of ownership is based on the number of shares owned compared to the total number of shares sold.

A corporation is a separate and distinct business entity that is responsible for itself. Upon formation, the corporation issues shares of stock to shareholders, the owners. A board of directors elected by the shareholders manages the corporation. This board then appoints officers of the corporation to handle the day-to-day affairs of the company. In essence, the board members represent the interests of the shareholders in the company operations.

# The Business Plan

The Small Business Association defines a business plan as

*A business plan precisely defines your business, identifies your goals, and serves as your firm's resume. The basic components include a current and pro forma balance sheet, an income statement, and a cash flow analysis. It helps you allocate resources properly, handle unforeseen complications, and make good business decisions. Because it provides specific and organized information about your company and how you will repay borrowed money, a good business plan is a crucial part of any loan application. Additionally, it informs sales personnel, suppliers, and others about your operations and goals.*

Just as a builder won't begin construction without a blueprint, eager spa owners shouldn't rush into new ventures without a business plan. You need a business plan if you are opening a spa. A business plan is like a map for a traveler. Without it, you are traveling blind. If you don't

> ### Smart Tip
> Tip...
>
> A business plan should be a living, breathing, ever-changing document. The road map for your business will be constantly changing as you meet challenges in your spa. You will frequently review and update your business plan. The right length of the plan depends on the nature and purpose of the plan. It should not be longer than 50 pages.

know where you are going, you probably won't reach your ultimate destination. A business plan clearly explains just what you intend to do and how you intend to do it. It is the guidebook for your spa business to follow.

# Why Do You Need a Business Plan?

Everyone needs a business plan. You need a business plan if you are applying for a business loan. Most banks require it, and even those that do not strictly require it, expect it. They expect it to be a summary of the business, with some predictable key points. You need a business plan if you are working with partners. The business plan defines agreements between partners about what's going to happen. You need a business plan to set a value on a business for sale or legal purposes or to sell a business. You need a business plan to communicate with a management team. How do you know where you are in business without establishing where you started and where you intended to go? How can people commit to a plan they can't see? You need a business plan if you are looking for business investments. Investors look to the business plan to define and explain your business. The plan will not get you the investment, but not having a plan will likely mean that you will not get your investment.

- You need a business plan if you are applying for a business loan. Most banks require it, and even those that do not strictly require it, expect it. They expect it to be a summary of the business, with some predictable key points.
- You need a business plan if you are working with partners. The business plan defines agreements between partners about what's going to happen.
- You need a business plan to set a value on a business for sale or legal purposes or to sell a business.
- You need a business plan to communicate with a management team. How do you know where you are in business without establishing where you started and where you intended to go? How can people commit to a plan they can't see?
- You need a business plan if you are looking for business investments. Investors look to the business plan to define and explain your business. The plan will not get you the investment, but not having a plan will likely mean that you will not get your investment.

# Tips for Writing Business Plans

- Is the plan simple and easy to understand? Does it communicate its contents easily and practically?
- Take the time to make the important points easily understood.
- Is the plan realistic? Are the sales goals, expense budgets, and milestone dates realistic?
- Is the plan complete? Does it include all the necessary elements?

# Business Plan Outline

○ *Cover Letter.* The cover letter should be personally addressed to the recipient by name, title, company, address, and current date.

○ *Table of Contents.* The table of contents allows the reader to go directly to a specific section. It presents the business plan as well organized.

○ *Executive Summary.* The executive summary is often the only section a potential investor will read. It is usually a one- to two-page summary presented at the beginning of the business plan, but written at the very end of preparing the business plan itself. It contains the highlights that will allow the reader to get a feel for the key elements covered in the remaining pages of the business plan.

○ *Business Description.* The business description explains your service idea and how it meets the needs of your market. It should be very brief and tightly focused to address how the proposed products or services will save customers and clients' time, money, and energy, and make their lives better. What problems will it solve? How will it reduce the stress in people's lives?

○ *Company Management and History.* For start-up businesses, there will be no history to discuss, but this section will allow you to emphasize the background skills that management is bringing to the company.

○ *Description of the Product or Service.* Lenders and investors want to know more about what makes this product or service sought after by the customer or client, and what makes it better than existing products or services in the market.

○ *Competition.* Who are the established spas already selling services similar to yours? What are they doing right and what can you do better? This section of the business plan allows the reader to gain confidence in your knowledge of the market and how well you have researched and checked out the competition and the potential for change.

○ *Marketing Plan.* Here is where you must document the benefits your customer gets from buying your product or service. It is important to be able to give statistics and cite studies that demonstrate the size of the market and any potential markets that can be looked upon for future expansion. In this section, it must be made very clear why the market would want your product or service compared to others provided by your competitors.

○ *Financial Data.* The financial data includes the previous year's financial statements or for start-ups, projections. The financial projections should include a projected balance sheet for the next two years and profit and loss and cash flow statements for the next two years.

○ *Appendix.* The appendix is an area where you will include the resumes of the owner and key management people. The resumes should have such information as employment background, education, experience, skills, any special awards, and areas of expertise.

▲

- Don't underestimate your competition. Assess your competitors within the business plan.
- Is the plan specific? Are its objectives concrete and measurable? Does it include specific actions and activities, each with specific dates of completion, specific persons responsible, and specific budgets?
- Don't use obsolete data while analyzing a rapidly fluctuating marketplace.
- Avoid typos and spelling errors.
- It is important not to lie or mislead the reader by using false data or false projections.
- Create a financial section to organize the detailed financial charts, tables, and other supporting information.
- Don't present an opinion as fact without supporting information. Your personal beliefs should be kept to a minimum.

# Business Laws

Inquire into federal, state, county, and local government laws before you start your spa. The federal government requires you to pay federal taxes on all the money you earn. State governments sometimes enact laws regulating the practice of massage in the state. County governments keep track of business names and issue certificates to businesses allowing them to use a business name. Here are some business laws that you need to be mindful of, when starting your own spa:

- Professional licensing laws specifically regulate practice of spa treatments that can exist at the state, county, and local levels. These laws apply only to some states, some counties and some cities. Business licenses are usually required by city governments. Occasionally a county requires a business license too.
- When you open your spa you will need to be sure you are locating your office in an area that is zoned for your type of business; if not, you will be asked to shut down. Be aware of the zoning laws. The zones create different kinds of neighborhoods—business areas, residential areas, industrial areas, and areas of mixed usage.
- In addition to these business laws there may be local requirements for bathrooms, lighting, and signage use. Some local governments charge businesses a tax on business property. Others also charge a sewer tax, which may be based on water usage and plumbing.

# Insurance Coverage

Determining the level of coverage that best meets your business needs is an important one. The single most important factor in determining this aspect of running a business is how much risk you are willing and financially able to take. For specific information on insurance coverage you need to talk to a qualified insurance agent. Generally speaking, the types of insurance spa owners are likely to need include liability, malpractice, casualty, worker's compensation, and life/health/ disability insurance.

- *Property or casualty insurance.* Protects your business from physical property damage in the event of fire, theft, or other disasters.
- *Workers' compensation.* Covers employee medical and rehabilitation expenses as a result of injuries on the job. This type of insurance is mandatory and required by law in all states.
- *Liability insurance.* Protects your business from damages associated with negligence, accidents, or injuries.
- *Life, health, and disability insurance.* Provides direct benefits as a result of death, illness, or injury.
- *Malpractice insurance.* Protects you in the event of a lawsuit resulting from alleged negligence or errors and omission that result in harm or injury to your clients.

# Practical Tips for Starting a Spa

Operating a homebased business can give you the best of both worlds. Like all small business owners, you enjoy the satisfaction of being your own boss and being the person who makes the decisions.

But if you run your business out of your home, you also enjoy the benefits of being able to work flexible hours, of not having to commute, and certain tax advantages. In theory, you can run a successful business out of your home and have the flexibility to be there for your family, spending more time with your children or arranging your work schedule around your family's needs.

Starting any business requires planning and soul-searching, but there are particular aspects of your business operations that need to be considered carefully before you start a homebased business.

No wonder so many people are attracted to operating a homebased business. But is operating a homebased business right for you?

## Running a Home Spa: Pros and Cons

Working out of the home has become trendy these days. More and more people are doing it—and loving it, too. Many entrepreneurs choose to work from home, even when they don't have to. But, is a home spa for you?

There are many considerations to keep in mind when you are deciding whether it makes sense to operate your business from your home. Some of these considerations are financial, whereas others relate to the effects of working from home on your personal life.

## ADVANTAGES OF RUNNING A HOMEBASED SPA

**Stat Fact**
According to Sage Publications, the homebased business is a growing part of the U.S. economy, producing over *10 percent of all receipts of the small-business sector in 1996, and their numbers growing rapidly.*

Does working from home really save you money? In some ways, yes. You are already paying all the expenses on your home, whether or not you have your business there: the mortgage/rent, utilities, property taxes, maintenance, and a host of other costs are already paid. The main savings are in rent or mortgage. So, you can save the money you would spend on office space and put it back into your business.

Working at home is a 40-second commute from the kitchen to the office. You save one to four hours per day in commuting time, which provides more time for business. You can also work at night, after everyone else has gone to sleep. It can also allow you to be at home when your children get home from school, thereby saving on child care expenses. If you can discipline yourself well enough, having a home office will let you structure your day more efficiently around family needs.

There are tax advantages to having a home office. You may be able to deduct expenses associated with the office section of your house, which otherwise are not deductible. You are closer to your family, which allows for quality time at home with your spouse/partner/children. You might be able to rope family members into helping, on occasion.

## DISADVANTAGES OF RUNNING A HOME SPA

When you run a homebased spa, you are relatively isolated in your home office. A regular office provides contact with other business owners.

Your motivation may be curtailed. You can get sidetracked by personal projects such as cleaning the kitchen, answering personal phone calls, and watching television.

Running a homebased spa may affect your relationship with your neighbors. Your neighbors might not be as enthusiastic as you are about your new enterprise, especially if it results in increased traffic on what would otherwise be a quiet, residential, street. If you plan on having customers coming to your home office, you may want to discuss it with your neighbors first. You are not asking their permission; rather, you are simply informing them as a courtesy and encouraging them to bring any concerns to your attention immediately instead of going to the municipality to complain.

## Insurance and Zoning

If you are running a homebased spa, find out if your house insurance covers a business, too. If not, you may have to get a separate insurance policy to cover the loss of business assets in your home or to cover the interruption in your business if something catastrophic happens.

Zoning laws are an important consideration when running a homebased spa. The zoning of your neighborhood may be residential only and may not allow a business to operate. Check with your local zoning office to find out whether it is even possible for you to operate out of your home. You may have to pay extra fees or property taxes to the municipality in order to be able to operate a homebased business.

Before renting office space, you can test the water with a home business without incurring a lot of outside financial costs and obligations. If your idea takes off, you can always move to a regular office.

You will be on call most of the time. Even if you set parameters on your availability, it is probable that your customers will not always honor those limits. Since you are at home, they might drop in at their convenience to see if you are in for a manicure, pedicure, or facial. How would you handle such unexpected situations? If you are the type of person who wants to create a distinct separation between your home life and your working life, you may not want to have a home office.

You need to have the self-discipline to draw boundaries; if not, your home spa will not be successful. You have the freedom to sit on the couch and watch television, make chit chat on the phone, and mix household chores with your spa-related work. If you are not good at disciplining yourself to get things done by setting goals for yourself, a home spa may not be for you. Some people need the structure that an office away from home offers, in which case you may need to locate your spa elsewhere.

# Build or Buy?

Is it better to build a spa from the ground up or to purchase an existing spa? Each strategy has its pros and cons. The strategy that is right for you will depend partly on your motivation for owning a spa and partly on cash-flow considerations.

# Building a Business

Buying an existing business is usually the more expensive option. However, a business that is already up and running may provide you with profits and an income earlier, thus offsetting the initial cost.

When you start on your own, you start with nothing except an idea. You will need time mapping out that idea, working out cash-flow scenarios, doing market research, writing a business plan, and learning spa management techniques, among other things. It may take months or even years before you hit the break-even point, much less make a profit that you can put in your pocket.

The advantages of building a business from scratch are:

- As the spa owner you can design internal systems and décor the way you want them to work right from the start.
- It can be less expensive than buying an existing operation.
- There is no risk of acquiring a previous owner's liabilities or having to satisfy pre-existing warranties.
- You can select your staffing needs. You don't necessarily have to inherit employees from a previous owner.

The disadvantages of building a business from scratch are:

- It can take longer to generate profits than with an existing business.
- It can take a long time to build name recognition and goodwill with customers.
- There is much greater risk of failure than with a business that has a proven track record.
- It can be more difficult to attract investors. Because the venture does not exist yet, it will be riskier for them.

# Buying an Existing Business

Buying an existing business is less of a risk. You have had the opportunity to see the business in action, and you will be able to access financial records from previous years to determine growth rate, solvency, and profitability. You may also choose to buy a business if you want to quickly introduce a new service to an existing customer base before there are too many competitors in the market. For example, if you are buying a nail salon, you will already have an established client base.

Where do you look to see who is selling existing spas? Industry associations and trade publications are typically good places to begin searching for spa business opportunities. Visit their classified sections. The internet classifieds also list spas for sale. Attend professional functions and trade shows, and seek out those in the know who might be willing to assist you in your search. You might also consider using a business broker to act as your agent. Get in the habit of checking out the real estate classified sections on your own. This will keep you abreast of the cost of commercial retail space and square footage available. Conducting research online is another easy and anonymous way to access information quickly about spas for sale.

Th advantages of buying an existing business are:

- It can be easier to obtain external financing than if you build a business from scratch because the business has a track record.
- You can generate profits right from the purchase date.
- You can market your existing services to your new customer base.
- It is easier to manage an existing business model and fine tune it than to build it from scratch.
- You can continue the business with its established name recognition.

The disadvantages of buying an existing business are:

- If the previous owner has had a negative reputation, it will be difficult for you to change that image.
- The customers you are "buying" may have remained loyal to the business because of their ties to the previous owner and may not choose to stay on as customers when you take over.
- You may be inheriting the hidden headaches of the previous owner.
- It may take as long to reshape the business the way you want it as it would to have started a new business from scratch.

# Negotiating a Lease

Most owners will lease space at the start. A lease is a contract between you the spa owner and the landlord. A lease establishes the terms of using a specific space for a certain length of time. The lease price is typically based on dollars per square foot.

Before signing a lease agreement, look for items in a lease that give you flexibility and control. Avoid clauses that give power to the landlord and obligate you excessively. For example, your lease should include a statement that the space provided will be suitable for use as a professional spa service in terms of noise level, temperature control, parking, etc. This gives you a legal right to complain if the landlord fails to provide you with a quiet and warm spa environment.

If you have any doubts about the zoning for the location, put in the lease that it becomes void if the city refuses to approve zoning for a spa business at that location. Otherwise, you could be stuck with a lease on a space where you cannot operate.

You may also want to negotiate a lease that is renewable at your option. You don't know for sure that you will succeed in your business or that you will like the location. Give yourself the option to leave after a year or two. Simultaneously, give yourself the option to renew for a second and third year so that you know you will be able to enjoy the reward for your efforts if your business is successful. Having a lawyer look over the lease is a good idea. Get an informed and educated opinion before signing.

# Spiritual Tips for Opening a Spa

Building a strong, spiritual life can become a key component of your success as an entrepreneur. Start your day with a prayer of gratitude for another day. Draw in the morning's peace by taking a slow deep breath and meditation. Use a mindfulness meditation to slow down. Most successful entrepreneurs spend such time on meditation. Most of us are rushing through our lives without noticing that we are alive. Learn to focus on the here and now. Stay present.

Associate with people who care about you and share your values. This does not mean you don't reach out to other people, but don't spend time with people who don't share your values.

Honor yourself and your own feelings and ideas. Figure out who you are and then reject any other opinions that do not honor yours. They can affect your self-esteem and cause you fall by the way side. Having a strong spiritual foundation will enable you to avoid the many traps that others may set for you.

Most of all, ask the universe to support you.

## Believe in Yourself

If you want your spa to succeed, you must believe in yourself. Believing in yourself is a critical part of running any successful business. After all, if you lack the confidence in what you do, how can you expect others to believe in you? When you believe in yourself and invest the hard work required to making your dreams come true, these positive traits enhance your self-esteem and confidence, which subconsciously translate into the day-to-day handling of spa operations. Your employees respect you more, customers trust you more, and your business will thrive more.

Associate with people who affirm your goodness and not those who try to bring you down. Those who see that inner radiance in you feel secure about themselves while those who see negativity feel insecure about themselves. Cultivate relationships with the former as they will serve as stepping stones, not stumbling blocks.

# Stoic Resilience in the Face of Rejection

Rejection comes with the territory of becoming a spa owner. When you are running a spa, you are likely to get rejected in different areas of the business. There may be rejections from the local county, customers, landlords, neighbors, and bank officers. Initially rejections can be disappointing. After going through several, however, you will get used to it. The important thing is to not get discouraged. Use rejection to your advantage. It can bring you closer to running a successful spa business. Rejection needs to be taken as a sign of strength and hope, and not a reason to harbor vengeance. Use the word "no" to your advantage and transform it to "yes, I can."

Don't be discouraged by setbacks. The main thing is to not give up. Plant new seeds every day. Diversify your marketing efforts rather than concentrating only on one thing. Target groups of people from all walks of life. It may take time for people to start noticing your work, but if you keep toiling at it, the rewards will await you. Never let rejections turn your dreams to dust. Try hard and you will succeed. Yes, you can do it.

# Trappings of Success

Nothing breeds business interest faster than the smell of money. It is like sharks smelling blood for miles. They all love you when you are successful and avoid you like the plague when you are fallen. Your business success makes you a desirable business partner, speaker for public events, dinner date, and financial planning client. You will soon appear on everybody's mailing list; party invitations will pour in; sweet songs will pour into your ears from all corners; and the whole world will smile at you. All this is great, and you should enjoy the fruits of your labor. Remember, however, that you can become unknown again as quickly as you became a success. Running a spa business can be filled with numerous ups and downs.

As you move forward with your business, you will realize that some people will genuinely lend you a helping hand and wish you success while others will superficially wish you well but may not be as sincere toward your success as a spa owner. Sometimes it may be difficult to figure out who is sincere and who is not. Remember Orson Wells' classic *Touch of Evil*, "Behind the image lies the true motive"? Similarly, with time you will learn to penetrate beyond the outer image of people who come into your inner circle of trust and determine those who are sincere and those who are opportunists. Your fair weather friends will remain loyal to you as long as you have a fat checking account. Your faithful friends will get you through the dark times and encourage you to prosper when it is light again. Cultivate healthy relationships with people who affirm your goodness.

Success breeds success, but it also brings out opportunists who try to benefit from all your hard work and offer nothing in return. Determine early in your business relationships whether someone is trying to offer help, take help, or use you, and respond wisely.

Never forget who helped you when you first started out. Were there many colleagues and advisors or just a few when you were down? Some of you may have been alone during your years of struggle to becoming a successful spa owner. Many people who know you when you are becoming successful probably did not know you back when things were tough.

Handle the trappings of success wisely.

# Checklist for Opening a Day Spa

## 9–12 Months Before Opening

1. *Is your service easily marketable?* Starting a business that has a service needed by a large segment of the population is far easier than developing a new service and having to both familiarize potential customers with it and at the same time convince them that they need it.

2. *Can you make money?* Make sure that there is profit potential for your spa. For example, it may be difficult to earn a decent income concentrating only on braiding in your salon, and not offer haircuts, coloring, texturing, and styling. Incorporate a diverse treatment plan related to your field of operation.

3. *What are the barriers?* Some industries are more difficult than others to break into. How easy/difficult is it to break into the spa business? For example, if there is an Ayurveda resort in your area, starting a second one right next to it might not be such a good idea.

4. *Can your spa withstand downturns?* Determine if your spa is able to survive external changes and if it is adaptable. During dire economic times, people may not have money to spend on manicures and Botox. During such times, your spa can focus on basic services such as haircuts and beard trimmings. When times are good, you can promote luxury services such as pedicures, massages, and facials. Change with the times and go with the economic flow.

5. *Do you have patience?* Sometimes success as a spa owner comes only after a period of building a reputation in your community. Do things to become known and give your infant spa some time. As the French say, "Aie de la patience!" (Have patience.)

## 3–9 Months Before Opening

1. *Legal requirements.* Contact your local government for information about zoning and any regulations on health, fire, and police regulations. You must pay federal taxes, and often state and local, on all the money you earn. State governments sometimes enact laws regulating the practice of massage. County governments track business names and issue certificates to businesses allowing them to use a business name.

2. *Find a location.* Location, location, location. Find a place that is going to draw people, a place that does not offer too many services similar to yours, and is surrounded by a community with the disposable income to spend on spa services.

## Checklist for Opening a Day Spa, continued

3. *Run a home spa by your neighbors first.* Your neighbors might not be as enthusiastic as you are about your new enterprise, especially if it results in increased traffic volume. If you plan on having customers coming to your home office, you'll want to discuss it with your neighbors first.

4. *Negotiate a lease/buying office space.* You may also want to negotiate a lease that is renewable at your option. Give yourself the option to leave after a year and also give yourself the option to renew for a second and third year. Have a lawyer look over the lease.

### 6 Months Before Opening

1. *Change with the times.* Consumer tastes are ever-changing. If the rage last summer was Botox, next summer there may be a different anti-aging product. Keep on top of changes in the operating spa environment. It is important to continually analyze the environment in which your business operates and assess how you are positioned to take advantage of opportunities and deal with roadblocks.

    Stay on top of changes in the industry by reading industry publications and networking with other small business owners, both those in your particular industry and those who operate businesses in the same community as you. The more informed you are, the better you will be able to finance the future. Be flexible. Learn to adapt and change, while holding on to the good things of old-fashioned trends.

2. *Keep it coming.* One very serious and frequent mistake of spa owners is to concentrate only on today's work without considering where the work will come from tomorrow. As a small business owner, you have three heads: one that looks back to the past to learn from history, one that is focused on the here and now, and one that looks to the future. Prepare a plan in advance to keep the work coming in. Plant seeds continuously.

### 2–4 Weeks Before Opening Your Spa

1. *Register your spa name with your county.*
2. *Open a business checking account.*
3. *Obtain a new phone number for your spa.*
4. *Order stationery, business cards, and other promotional material to market your spa.*
5. *Buy/lease necessary spa equipment.*
6. *Notify the public of your grand opening and any introductory promotions you may be having.*

# 6

# Spa Management

**S**etting up any type of spa, whether it be day, medical, destination, or spiritual, entails an understanding of the logistics of what it takes to carry out a "pampering" industry. The multifaceted operational aspects of the spa business require an in-depth understanding of its complex dynamics in order to ensure a smooth operation and profitability.

Attention to the quality of the service delivered can make all the difference in impressing spa clients who are seeking superior healing experiences. As clients become more knowledgeable and demanding, the spa industry—and you—must progress and evolve in order to satisfy them.

There is a misconception that spa management revolves around hiring and scheduling. It is important to remember that managing a spa involves much more than that. Spa management covers three basic topics: building a business, managing a business, and doing what the business does. These three very different areas require different skills. You may not like all three. For example, you may enjoy giving stone massages but not bookkeeping. Not to worry. You can still become a successful spa manager through self-learning, hiring the right people, and making sound decisions.

The key is to be successful at spa management, which can play an important role in determining the profitability of your spa. The main components of spa management are:

- Smart staffing
- Employees
- Savvy interviewing
- Retaining massage therapists
- Knowing the customer
- Creating a happy office culture
- Hiring a trustworthy bookkeeper
- Using spa consultants
- Providing decent amenitites
- Having an eye on expansion

# Smart Staffing

Your spa's true assets are not money, equipment, or information, but the people working for you. Your staff is your single most valuable asset; they can make or break your business. The demand for qualified staff is a huge challenge in the booming spa industry. The importance of selecting the right personnel to ensure the success of your business cannot be emphasized enough. These are the people who will ultimately be standing toe-to-toe with your customers and bringing (or failing to bring) money into your spa business.

The greatest obstacles to your company's future growth and health can be to finding, growing, and maintaining quality human capital. Oftentimes, the most frequently overlooked business assets are the people you employ. Hiring the wrong employees could be a deadly mistake in the future of your spa.

Spas with comprehensive programs for employee recruiting, selection, and training, combined with sound incentive programs, have greater market value, higher annual sales, and higher profits per employee than those that do not, because of lower turnover and higher employee productivity.

When hiring new staff, seek the help of a qualified human resources consultant and a lawyer in order to formulate your interview questions carefully. If you are interested in doing drug testing, check the regulations in your state first. It is always advisable to have job-related application forms, interview questions, and job descriptions reviewed by a qualified business attorney who has a good understanding of employment laws. It is important to take these preliminary steps before hiring someone for your spa, even though it is fairly time consuming and financially costly.

# Seven Reasons Why You Should Select the Right People

1. It is much easier to make good hiring decisions than to deal with the hassles and legal entanglements that can result from poor hiring decisions and the loss of high-quality employees and customers. The time and effort you spend on the hiring process protects the health of the entire spa.

2. Smart investment in human capital gives you financial stability.

3. A high-quality, stable workforce offers you confidence about the long-term prospects of your business.

4. Choosing the wrong employee for the job costs you money, time, and energy. You will have to fire this wrong employee and find someone new, hire someone to pick up the slack, or interview new candidates for the vacant position. The loss of revenue and profit caused by losing an employee can be significant.

5. Bad employees chase away good customers. Poor employee performance leads to customer loss, lower sales, and less profit, especially in a hospitality industry like the spa.

6. You can be held legally accountable for your hiring decisions. This can cost you a lot of money in certain situations.

7. Good employees make management easier. Business owners who make good hiring decisions and retain top employees tend to be more successful and less stressed. Their workers know their jobs and fulfill their responsibilities efficiently even when the boss is not around. This also paves the way to creating a happy working environment both for the boss and for the employees.

# The Hiring Process

Think before you hire. First create your objectives for hiring an individual. Take a good look at your spa's needs, carefully define the job you want to fill, and determine what kind of employee can best fill the position. You should have identified what you want the employee to accomplish and what resulting benefit that employee will produce.

### STEP ONE: THINK BEFORE YOU HIRE

Take a good look at your spa's needs, carefully define the job you want to fill, and determine what kind of employee can best fill the position.

### STEP TWO: PREPARING THE JOB DESCRIPTION

A precise job description must be developed for each position. The job description should describe the areas or tasks the employee is responsible for, give a detailed compilation of performance standards for each task, and indicate the behavior expected from the employee. Employees must know what they will be held responsible for and against what standards their performance will be measured. The company then has a common point of reference, a common beginning from which measurements can begin.

The job descriptions should include the following elements:

- Job responsibilities and duties
- Essential job functions
- Expected level of performance
- Potential for advancement
- Compensation

### STEP THREE: LOCATE QUALIFIED APPLICANTS

Develop a recruiting plan and determine where you can find the best applicants to suit your needs.

If you have completed the pre-employment phase, you will have prepared a job description and performance standards. Now you need to set up procedures to guide the process. These will include setting up a selection team (if appropriate), identifying a beginning and ending date for the recruitment process (as well as an employment start date), selecting appropriate media to post the opening, and preparing written material such as the employment application, job announcement, and interview questions. Be sure the process is written down and followed to assure consistency with each candidate.

## STEP FOUR: IDENTIFYING SOURCES OF QUALIFIED CANDIDATES

Select the appropriate media to post your job opening. Current employee search methods include personal contacts, school career planning and placement offices, employers, classified ads, internet, professional associations, labor unions, and private employment agencies. Here are some ways to seek the right candidates for your job openings:

**Stat Fact**

According to the Bureau of Labor Statistics' (www.bls.gov) *Occupational Outlook Handbook,* 80 percent of available jobs are never advertised, and over half of all employees get their jobs through networking and personal contacts.

- *Print advertisements.* Create an accurate, compelling ad that will generate the response you need from qualified candidates.
- *Magazines.* Spa trade publications are especially good at reaching qualified candidates.
- *Newspapers.* This is the traditional source for classified ads. If you want a local person, use local papers with wide circulation in the surrounding area.
- *Visiting massage therapy schools.* Give a lecture about your spa, post advertisements in the school bulletin board, and promote your spa at massage therapy institutions.
- *Internet postings.* Internet advertising is the most current method of seeking qualified candidates.
- *Referral programs.* Word-of-mouth or employee referral can be the most effective means of attracting new qualified recruits. Referral programs are usually the most cost-efficient because candidates who learn about a company through an existing employee tend to be a better fit and stay with the business longer.

## STEP FIVE: INTERVIEW CANDIDATES AND SELECT YOUR NEW EMPLOYEE

Create a step-by-step interviewing process that helps you to choose the best candidate (See Savvy Interviewing on page 54).

## STEP SIX: REWARD AND KEEP TOP EMPLOYEES

The key is to hold onto the good employees who draw customers and excel at what they do. Avoiding rapid turnover of employees is a sign of smart staffing. Good selection of employees can ensure many rewards for your business.

# Employees

Recruiting and keeping the right employees matters. Be aware of what types of retention efforts keep your best employees on board. According to Human Resources.com the following three are the most common programs employers are using to retain employees:

1. Tuition reimbursement is provided by 62 percent of employers.
2. Competitive vacation and holiday benefits are offered by 60 percent of employers.
3. Competitive salaries are offered by 59 percent of employers.

## Training Your Employees

Coaching is a critical component of training your employees. Ideally, coaching or orientation should begin on every new employee's first day on the job and continue for as long as that person works in your spa. As the owner, you also have to be there to watch and listen as your employees first try the basic components of the task and then the complete task. To be an effective coach, you need to know the game yourself. This includes knowing, understanding, and demonstrating the specific skill or behavior you are trying to teach.

Team members need to receive regular training sessions on all the treatments and products offered at your spa. It never hurts to have a refresher course on important details of products and services offered, as well as those not offered at the spa. This gives employees a well-rounded knowledge of the industry, which will come across in positive ways as they mingle with clients.

Benefits of employee training and development include reduced employee turnover, increased job satisfaction and morale among employees, increased innovation in spa treatments, enhanced spa image, increased employee motivation, increased efficiencies in processes resulting in financial gain, and effective damage control in negative publicity.

## Strategies for Evaluating Employee Progress

Employee progress must be evaluated on a continuous basis, and not as a one-time thing. Employees must have clear job descriptions to

### Stat Fact

Human Resources.com employees cited the following three top reasons they would begin searching for a new job:

1. Seek better compensation and benefits: 53 percent.
2. Dissatisfaction with potential career development: 35 percent.
3. Ready for a new experience: 32 percent.

which they are held accountable. Their job descriptions must be refreshed periodically. The performance and potential of each employee must be reviewed on a periodic basis with a supervisor or manager. By doing so, the personal and professional development of employees gets recognized as a vital activity. It also makes employees feel like they are an important part of the spa and gives incentives for providing superior customer service to clients.

The management staff needs to discuss development on a regular basis with employees. During this process the management must take input from employees on improving the quality of work life into serious consideration. Customer satisfaction must be assessed on a regular basis as well. Their feedback must be discussed with spa staff.

## How to Retain Massage Therapists

Retention of massage therapists, as opposed to other spa technicians, is a common concern among most spa owners. Unlike other areas in the industry, massage therapists tend to get burnt out more easily. Consequently, there is a rapid turnover of massage therapists. Take, for example, a routine working day of a massage therapist versus an esthetician. A massage therapist working in a spa could literally find herself booked solid, doing nothing but the same type of one-hour massage for the duration of her shift. A massage therapist could be giving back massages for five hours at a stretch. An esthetician, on the other hand, has a wider range of popular services that he will be booked for during a shift. Estheticians frequently do lash tints, makeup application, waxing, beauty consultations, and other types of face and body treatments. The workload of a massage therapist is more repetitive than this.

The type of physical work required of a massage therapist versus an esthetician is much more taxing. A massage therapist must commit the whole of her body, oftentimes engaging multiple muscle groups. In deep-tissue massage, in particular, a great deal of strength, endurance, and ongoing physical activity is required of the therapist. Moreover, the same areas of the hands, wrists, and arms are used repetitively. For example, an Ayurveda oil massage requires much more intense muscle usage on the part of the therapist than a nail trimming by an esthetician. At some point for many therapists, this sort of routine becomes like working on an assembly line. Estheticians on the other hand do mostly above-the-waist work, which requires a lighter touch. The movements are more varied, which decreases overuse injuries.

As a spa owner, you can take some steps to avoid the rapid turnover of massage therapists. Be flexible with a massage therapist's weekly or daily workload. Whereas an esthetician may work 40 hours a week, a massage therapist can work half that much because the physical demands are more. A second step is to cross-train massage therapists in other treatments such as hydrotherapy and machine-based services.

Rotate them into the front desk shifts and the gift shop, thereby helping to break the monotony of their work routine. This will enable massage therapists to spend quality time with spa guests and lighten their physical load.

Make your work place a pleasant environment for massage therapists. Showing appreciation for a job well done, creating variety in their workloads, and treating each massage therapist's needs as top priority will help you retain them.

# Savvy Interviewing

There are three goals when conducting an employment interview:

1. To develop an accurate picture of the job for which you are hiring and communicate that to each applicant.
2. To collect enough information on the applicant to make an informed decision about hiring a new employee.
3. To produce a positive and accurate picture of the spa, one that will impress applicants and help them decide to work for you.

The job interview gives the potential employee and potential spa employer a chance to learn more about each other. Developing the right set of questions can make a tremendous difference in the types of employees that you hire.

There are several types of interviews:

- *Screening interview*. This is used to quickly and efficiently eliminate unqualified or overpriced candidates. Conducted by professional interviewers, recruiters, or personnel representatives seeking information regarding educational and experiential background using a highly structured question and answer format.

- *Selection interview*. This type of interview is often used after some type of screening process. Usually conducted by a professional practitioner who will be the candidate's supervisor. It is generally less formal and less structured than the screening interview. Questions tend to be open-ended with subsequent questions based upon candidate's responses to previous questions.

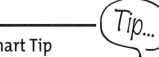

## Smart Tip

The goal of the interviewer is to

1. promote the organization and attract the best possible candidate.
2. gather information about the candidate.
3. assess how well the candidate's qualifications match the job requirements.
4. determine whether the candidate will fit in with the organization and the staff.

- *Search committee or board interview.* A group that consists of many interviewers and one candidate. Used by business and industry for selection of high level corporate officers. Typical of a selection committee search in higher education.
- *Group interview.* A group consists of many candidates and one or more interviewers. Frequently used as a screening procedure by smaller companies and by graduate and professional schools. Used to assess leadership skills and ability to work in groups.

Take a look at the sample interview questions to consider when preparing for a job interview. Some of the answers to interview questions can be filled out after the screening interview, before the employee comes in.

## Sample Interview Questions

### Questions about Previous Jobs

What were your start and end dates of employment?

What was your specific title? Duties? Responsibilities?

What was your starting and ending pay?

What was your specific reason for leaving?

### Questions about Present Job

What are you looking for in a job?

What do you look for in a company that you would like to work for?

Why should I hire you?

Why do you want to work in my spa?

What training or qualifications do you have for a job like this?

What do you think will be the most challenging aspect of this job? How will you handle that aspect?

What are your income expectations from this job?

### Questions about Attitudes

What is the biggest challenge you have faced? How did you handle it?

How long will it take for you to make a positive contribution here?

What do you expect from your employer?

Describe your ideal supervisor.

What makes a job enjoyable for you?

What do you want out of this job?

## Sample Interview Questions

What do you consider important in a job?

From whom have you learned the most?

Tell me about a responsibility you have enjoyed.

How do you define a successful career?

What is more important to you: the salary or the job itself?

What do you think determines a person's progress in a spa like ours?

### Questions on Teamwork

What has been your greatest accomplishment as a member of a team?

Do you prefer working alone or in a group?

When working in a group, what role do you prefer?

How would your teammates describe your style when working together?

### Questions on Communication and Interpersonal Skills

Communication skills are important in this job; please tell me your two biggest strengths as communicator.

What is your biggest strength in dealing with people?

What type of person is the hardest for you to get along with?

How did you get along with a former boss?

Tell me about a work situation that required excellent communication skills.

What sort of a person do you enjoy working for?

Tell me about a time when you had to make an unpopular decision.

Tell me about a time when you best handled an irate customer.

# Background Checks and References

Always conduct a background check before hiring. There are licensed professionals who can do this for you, or ask your lawyer. Especially in a people industry like spas, the importance of background checks cannot be emphasized enough. A reference check must be performed in a deliberate fashion. Questions asked of business and/or professional references should be related exclusively to past job performance.

Some sample reference questions are:

- How long did _____ work for you?
- Did he hold other positions within the company?
- How would you describe her work ethic?
- Given the opportunity would you hire him again?
- What reservations should I have about hiring her?
- Who else within your organization could comment on his performance?
- What were her reasons for leaving?

# Know the Customer

You have seen slogans like "We are a customer-driven company," "The customer is king," and "Customers are the life blood." The question is how many businesses live up to these demanding slogans?

If you want to be a savvy spa owner, you need to be able to have a keen ability to foresee what customers want even before they are aware of it. You need to anticipate customer needs and wants and provide those services to meet their satisfaction. No spa business can function effectively without a clear view of what prospective customers want. An understanding of competition, perception, product, and pricing may enable a business to keep its customers, but the key is customer service, which is everyone's responsibility.

Selling beef products in a vegetarian store is useless from a marketing point of view. Similarly, marketing your spa services and products to a population that does not want them is futile. The lesson here is to identify your customers. Many will give you all the praise in the world but not draw in business. Be picky and select clients who are likely to spend money on your spa services.

When you don't know who your likely customers are, the result is a scattergun marketing approach. Targeted marketing on the other hand makes you focus on the people most likely to purchase what your spa has to offer. Target marketing does not waste time, money, and effort approaching people who are not good prospects. As a result, you get much better results from your marketing efforts. The types of results you get vary widely from situation to situation, but you will always find target marketing a more manageable and efficient effort than the scattergun approach.

Customers are the ultimate driving force of your spa. A sound business is always centered around its customers. In essence, your customer is your boss. Customers dictate to a large extent how you should steer your business. The purpose of your spa is to gain and keep customers. Without customers in sufficient and steady numbers, you cannot run a spa business on a long-term basis. Keeping customers happy is good business and your best defense against competition. If your spa keeps your customers happy, they remain loyal and will seek your services more often. Happy customers are willing to pay extra for the additional satisfaction they get from a business.

In order to gauge how happy customers are with your spa service, look at your quality of service and service design. For example, a Shiatsu treatment that immediately alleviates a person's pain or the choice of spa music that puts the client into the right mood during a manicure treatment are well integrated systems to which consumers immediately respond favorably.

One of the key success elements of spa management is visualization. Periodically, the staff must visualize themselves as "the client." Visualization must be encouraged and constantly reinforced at all levels of spa operations—from the front desk team members to the spa attendants, skin care specialists, physicians, gift shop clerk, and therapists. Each staff member shares responsibility for ensuring a memorable and pleasant spa experience for clients. Encourage each team member to analyze the spa's service by asking a few basic questions such as :

- How do I feel upon entering the spa for the first time?
- How would I like to be greeted upon entering the spa?

# Customer Satisfaction

**C**ustomer satisfaction is the basic entry point of a sound business practice. Your spa should provide good satisfaction to all customers. To build satisfaction, you must earn it. Here are some tips:

- ❍ Set high standards for your spa.
- ❍ Weigh the advantages and disadvantages of maintaining relationships with a client who is consistently creating problems for your establishment.
- ❍ If a customer is dissatisfied with your spa service, mend the relationship right away whenever possible.
- ❍ Anticipate your customers expectations.
- ❍ Make customer satisfaction everybody's business.
- ❍ Strive to create and manage customers' expectations.
- ❍ Design your spa services to maximize customer satisfaction. Make it easy on your customer.

- What kind of music, sculpture, fragrance, and lighting would I like to experience as I enter the spa?
- What can I do to enhance the client's overall spa experience?

# Difficult Customers and Tricky Issues

Clients come in all types. Some require a great deal of tact, diplomacy, patience, and skill. As a spa owner, you need to be able to handle these difficult customers gently but firmly. Some customers can be problematic and will complain about anything that you do. You need to train your staff to handle such situations diplomatically. Emphasize the need to maintain and enforce appropriate boundaries.

Sometimes clients expect the massage therapists to be their marriage counselor, physician, or psychologist. Remind your therapists that they are none of these. They need to draw boundaries with clients and not become too intimate with their clients' private lives. They should not venture beyond the realm of their spa licenses. They can listen to their clients' internal struggles but need to remain impartial and not offer advice.

# Return Policy

Creating a return customer base is one of the best ways to establish customer loyalty. Customer loyalty is the practice of finding, attracting, and retaining spa customers. Any customer loyalty program must factor in the front line of the business. It is the point of contact between customer and employee that sets the foundation of repeat business.

### ACHIEVING 99 PERCENT GUEST RETENTION

The customer marketing function should be viewed as a two-part process: (1) getting customers and (2) retaining customers. Sales budgets, advertising campaigns, and promotional efforts usually take a significant percentage of a company's operating budget to attract new customers. The average American company spends six times more money on efforts to attract new customers than it does on efforts designed to nurture and keep its existing customers. Few spa owners, however, engage in aggressive, well-constructed strategies of retention-oriented marketing to keep customers happy.

Happy customers act like a volunteer sales force. They make referrals to friends, relatives, and colleagues. It is easier to make a repeat sale than it is to open a new account. You don't have to spend as much time, energy, and resources persuading customers to try your treatments. The question is no longer why the customer should visit your spa, rather the focus is on what services/products should you offer your existing customers and how frequently they should visit you.

Ask your customers on a regular basis how you are doing, how you can serve them better, what they perceive are your strengths and weaknesses, who they regard as your competition, and why. The goal of talking with your customers is for you to formulate a strategy for keeping these hard-earned clients.

Management communication with frontline employees and customers is key to achieving customer retention. The management staff spends most of its time behind the scenes and, therefore, may not have firsthand knowledge of what is going on. Frontline employees like the receptionist, gift shop clerk, and massage therapists, on the other hand, are in regular contact with customers. As a result, they know a great deal more about customers' perceptions, expectations, and levels of satisfaction than the management does. In too many spas, healthy communication between frontline employees and management has been damaged. When these channels of communication are closed or inadequate, management lacks key feedback about problems occurring in service delivery as well as critical information about changing customer expectations. This can gravely affect a spa business.

To truly understand and appreciate customers' needs and expectations, spa owners should experience firsthand what really happens in the field. As a spa owner, spend some time dealing with customers face-to-face. As often as possible, put yourself in the shoes of frontline employees and see what it is like. This is the best test for studying customers and retaining them.

Sometimes there is a gap between what customers expect and what management presumes they want. This often happens because spas overlook or don't fully understand customers' perceptions and expectations. An internally directed focus assumes that the spa owner knows what customers *should* want. This orientation often leads to providing services that do not match customers' expectations. In spite of a strong commitment and sincere desire to provide quality service, many spas fall dramatically short of the mark, usually because they have an internally directed rather than an externally directed focus.

Being customer driven doesn't mean driving yourself to bankruptcy. As a spa owner, you must be able to assess your customer base. Certain customers are just not worth it. Let them go. Effectively "fire" customers who are hurting your spa image. Some may ask for free treatments consistently because they were not satisfied with what you offered them. Such customers can cause a loss of business. If you find that the customers you are attracting through your marketing efforts are not making you successful, you need to disconnect from the relationship that exists between the business and the customer, and redefine that relationship. You may have to fire some of your existing problematic customers and return them to the marketplace. This will create room for you to approach new customers. Know when to walk away from a customer.

## INCREASING CUSTOMER RETENTION

- *Be reliable*. Customers want consistent performance. Key ways to provide reliability are to do what you say you are going to do, stick to deadlines, and get it right the first time. You rarely get a second chance to create a first impression.

- *Select frontline employees carefully*. Spas oriented toward customer service should have customer-friendly people in frontline positions. Great care should be exercised in selecting prospective employees based on their personality traits, honesty, and hard work ethics.

- *Be credible*. Earn your customers' trust. They want the services that they receive to be free of danger, risk, and doubt.

- *Have empathy*. Being empathetic means putting yourself in the shoes of your customer. Ask yourself the question, would you do business with your spa?

- *Be responsive*. Being responsive requires being available, accessible, and willing to help customers whenever they have a problem. Make yourself available to your customer.

- *Provide sufficient employee training*. Customers want to be served by knowledgeable and efficient employees. Thus, employees should be well trained before interacting with customers. This should not be viewed as a one-time entrance requirement. Regular training sessions are needed to keep employees updated on new policies and procedures, new product features and benefits, competition, customer needs, new programs, and developments in other parts of the spa.

## EMPLOYEE ROLE IN CUSTOMER RETENTION

The key metric to track in your spa customer loyalty program is customer retention. How many customers are defecting? How many clients are retained? Measuring customer retention is half the battle. Your staff must be rewarded for retention. Your small business doesn't have to be like big corporations who talk retention but only reward sales people for bringing in new customers.

Any small business wishing to start a customer loyalty initiative needs first to identify important customers and understand their customers' behaviors. Equally vital is to know your profit margins. Don't offer discounts until you know the impact on your bottom line.

Part of customer loyalty and retention are encouraging employees to maintain regular contact with your most profitable customers. Communication with your best customers should take the form of showing your appreciation and providing new learning experiences to add value to your customer's life. Train spa employees to send special thank-you notes, surprise gifts, and regular communications such as newsletters to connect with them.

The management staff must regularly meet with spa employees who work directly with customers. During these meetings, concerns and complaints must be discussed.

Depending on the size of the spa, individual managers or supervisors must be held responsible for the loss of customers resulting from inadequate customer service. Supervisors must be responsible for handling customer complaints, which must be addressed promptly. Customer complaints must be entered in a complaint/concern log. The owner must review this log regularly and address issues as necessary.

# Creating a Happy Office Culture

The reality is this: most workplaces do not have happy office cultures. Most people have worked in office environments where they have dreaded going to work every morning. Such environments are not mentally healthy places to work in.

Creating a happy office culture needs to be a priority for every spa owner. If your employees are happy, that will come across to the clients as well, making them want to return to your spa and give you their money. It is very important to cultivate employer-employee relationships every day, but it is especially crucial when things become hectic. Do simple, special things, like treating your staff to lunch when they are slammed, recognizing their birthdays with a cake, and offering praise when it is due. Offer bonus massages to your staff. For example, make it a rule that employees can receive regular spa treatments free of charge, at least two per month. Such incentives actually help your business. When team members experience treatments, they can discuss the procedures firsthand with clients.

Most spa owners would agree that when it comes to creating an efficient and happy staff, communication is key. Be open with your employees and conduct regular meetings to ensure the entire team stays on the same page regarding staffing issues, policies, community events, and marketing tactics. When you are open and honest with your team members, you find that oftentimes they are upfront with you as well. Always remember, if your spa is doing well, it is because you are working with your team, not alone.

# Hiring a Trustworthy Bookkeeper

Bookkeepers are the gatekeepers; they control who enters and exits the spa premises in the vital financial areas of the business. If you decide to do the bookkeeping on your own, go for it. If you hire someone else, follow the same steps as you do when hiring other employees.

Hiring a trustworthy bookkeeper is critical to the success or failure of your spa. You may have heard horror stories of bookkeepers embezzling money, time, and resources from business owners. Avoid giving sole authority and ensuring complete trust to your bookkeeper. Have an internal oversight system whereby the work quota done by the bookkeeper is shared by another staff member. Ideally, the bookkeeper should not have sole authority on decision-making matters, writing checks, and handling invoices, no matter how trustworthy he or she may be. When it comes to money, always have several people overseeing one another.

# Spa Consultants

A spa's first impression may be your client's last. The spa image that you create for your clients is critical for the success or failure of your business.

A spa differs from all other beauty businesses principally through the implied promise that the total experience of being there—everything from the initial greeting to checkout—will be exceptionally serene.

In the world of human emotions, joys are soon forgotten while disappointments run long and deep. Clients tend to remember the disappointments of a spa experience more than the joyful moments. Pay careful attention to the small, seemingly insignificant and yet critically important details that make a spa a place of relaxation for those that seek them out.

Here's a partial list of things that happy spa customers remember most:

- warm smiles and handshakes (emotional feelings of acceptance, safety, and belonging)
- instructions and directions around the spa environment
- intimacy
- cleanliness and order
- mood and energy
- sensitivity to unspoken needs. For example in a nonverbal way a client might indicate that she is tired. The therapist needs to be able to sense this.
- consistency
- appreciation

A spa consultant helps you to create the right environment to leave your clients feeling happy and content. From feasibility to conceptual development, to equipment selection, to turn-key staffing and management services, a spa consultant can assist every step of the way.

Spa consultants can help you in architectural plans, web design, on-site management, business plan writing, marketing, selecting the right music, and introducing the right cuisine to clients, among other areas.

Spa consultants are realists. And realists are not often the most popular guests at the cocktail party. They don't live in denial, but expose the nudity of a problem at hand. A spa consultant will tell you if the design you have in mind is appropriate, if your cuisine is driving away guests, and if the music at the reception is too painful for clients to hear. They will tell you things that will help you to improve your business. If your prospects for profit making are bleak, they will tell you that as well. You must set aside emotion in order to make sound decisions regarding your spa business, and a spa consultant does this task.

The spa consultant wants to help you. He/she wants to see you achieve personal satisfaction as well as lasting success. When you decide to bring in the skills of a consultant you should be absolutely committed to implementing the systems and tools you are paying for. Spa consultants may charge anywhere from $500 to $5,000 per day depending on the project or their experience; this is not money you can afford to waste. The fees of a spa consultant, even at the top end of the scale, may pale when compared to the cost efficiency and revenue generating benefits of successfully integrated programs or systems.

Remember, the consultant's fee is short-term expense while the benefits of their work may be in effect for the lifetime of your company. A $20,000 consultant fee may translate into hundreds of thousands of dollars in otherwise undiscovered revenue or gross profit. It's important not to focus on the upfront cost of the consultant but rather on the long term benefits. You must think of your consulting relationship as a business investment, one probably of more critical value than any other feature of your spa.

Who needs a spa consultant? If you are thinking about starting a spa, need remodeling on an existing spa, if your spa is heading towards bankruptcy, if you are not achieving the financial goals that you set for yourself, or need help with spa management, contacting a spa consultant may be a good idea (if you can afford it of course).

# What to Look for in a Consultant

- Talk to the consultant's current and former clients without giving the consultant time to prepare them.
- Ask the clients if they would re-hire that same consultant.
- Ask the client how the consultant handled certain difficult situations in the process.
- In case something goes wrong in the plan, does the consultant have a strong backup system to ensure the continuity of the process?

- Did the consultant stick to the promises or did he go over or under budget? What were the outcomes versus the promises?
- Talk to suppliers that the consultant works with. Ask about the consultant's ethical and professional practice.
- What is the financial background of the consultant?
- For how many corporate clients are they currently on retainer?

Although spa consultants may promise you a lot of things, it is important to cast a critical eye on their promises of savings. The reality is that no consultants, on their own, can actually save you money. A consultant provides advice, methodology, and recommendations based upon experience and expertise in a given discipline. What spa owners then do with that input is what can save them money.

There are many scam consultants out there. Some of them are out-of-work con artists who print business cards, put on a good suit, talk persuasively, and create an attractive web site on spa consulting services. They have good marketing and persuasive skills but lack the knowledge, training, and experience needed to run a spa consulting service. Others may be experienced in other fields such as hotels, hospitals, and residential homes, but not in the spa industry. So, beware of those who say they are spa consultants.

# Linens 'n Things

Apart from the managerial details of hiring the right employees and creating customer satisfaction, there are other details of spa management that define the line between mediocre and exceptional service that can make or break your spa. Introducing the right linens is one of the most critical, but by no means the only vital service need.

Don't wash your dirty linen in public. Airing your dirty laundry for clients to see and smell is definitely a no-no. Washers, dryers, and housekeeping supplies should be kept hidden from the client's view. Treatment rooms should contain hampers that are unobtrusive. If necessary, use a linen spray on soiled garments to avoid a foul odor. Always use clean linen in your nail salon, hair salon, massage beds, and clinics. They *do* make a big difference.

Should you hire a laundry service or do it yourself? Doing laundry yourself can cut down costs dramatically, especially if your spa is a small operation. However, if you hire a service, you don't have to have a washer and dryer in your spa. Trips to the laundry can be very wearing when you are taking several loads per week. If your spa is running smoothly and you can afford it, it may be in your interest to hire a professional service. Cleanliness is indeed next to godliness in the spa business.

The quality of your sheets and towels is another subtle factor that can make a big difference. Select sheets that give optimum comfort to guests. The quality and comfort of sheets is determined by the thread count, the number of threads used per square inch of the fabric. A higher thread count means a softer sheet. The fabric composition plays a role, too. The higher the percentage of cotton, the softer the sheet; the higher the percentage of polyester, the coarser the sheet.

Towels come in direct contact with clients bodies. Therefore, comfort is key. You may want to create a luxurious impression by using colorful linens with a lush texture. Consider using embroidery to sew the name of your spa on towels and sheets. This can serve as a marketing tool as well.

Clean facilities are vital to your spa business. If you just gave a haircut to a customer, first sweep the floor before inviting your next customer to the seat. If oil has dripped on the floor after giving a client an Indian head massage, mop it up before moving to the next customer.

The tub and drain should always be free of hair. Having hair from a previous guest leaves a powerful negative imprint that might make you lose valuable customers. Always have fresh soap for new guests. Don't keep used soap.

Introduce a gentle aromatic scent in your spa. Introducing live potted plants such as lavender or aloe vera can also create soothing and healing sensations for spa guests.

# An Eye on Expansion

Once you have had proven success with your business model, you may think about how much more profit you can make using your entrepreneurial skills. How do you know whether expanding your business makes financial sense? The decision process is much the same as the one you followed for starting your business in the first place.

Once your business has a record of financial success, your financing options widen. Those who seemed reticent to lend to you when you were just starting out may be warming up to the investment possibilities as you plan your expansion. Before you seek financing for the new operations, spend time updating your business plan, refining your cash flow forecasts, and doing market research. You can expand your spa at the local, national, or even international levels.

Having a trustworthy local consultant with knowledge about the spa industry can be a big help when expanding your spa business overseas.

# 7

# Using the Net to Catch Fish:
## Cyber Marketing

The internet is an exciting and potentially beneficial tool for your spa. With 69 percent of adults in the United States accessing the web, the internet has revolutionized how businesses operate, market, and communicate. Internet usage has exploded during the last few years, becoming the media of choice for many people seeking product and service information. The easiest and most cost-effective way to disperse your message is internet or cyber marketing.

# Spas and the Internet

A new study on spa travelers says the number-one source of information for planning a spa vacation is the web. According to a study sponsored by the International Spa Association and the Canadian Tourism Commission, 62 percent of Americans use web sites to plan their spa vacations, 60 percent follow recommendations from family and friends, and 33 percent use spa and travel guidebooks. Not only can a web site reach more clients, but it is also the face of your business online, and often the very first impression you present to potential new clients.

The Travel Industry Association of America (TIA) released its annual Travelers' Use of the Internet study in December 2003. The study shows an increase in the number of people using the internet to research and book travel. TIA found that 30 percent of the adult U.S. population (63.8 million) consult the web for travel information. Online travelers surf to two or more travel web sites, spending an average of 37 minutes. They research and compare prices, check schedules, and book trips. The number of people actually booking online increased by 8 percent over 2002 and grew to 42.2 million people in 2003. Within this group of online travelers, 32 million people made travel arrangements exclusively through the internet (a figure expected to grow, according to the TIA). Ten million travelers responded to e-mail campaigns, causing the TIA to believe that e-mail campaigns are stimulating unplanned travel. According to Internet World Statistics (www.internetworldstats.com) in the most recent 2007 report, an estimated 232, 057, 067 people in North America use the internet, approximately 69.4 percent of the total population.

## Web Sites

As a marketing tool, your web site provides measurable results unlike any other media. For example, you can track the number of visitors and the time they spend on any specific page, and you can monitor search terms that visitors use to find your web site. Your web service provider has the ability to determine exactly how many visitors, or hits, your site receives in any given period, even to the hour. After a few months, review the hit statistics to determine whether or not your web site is working for you. This information can be useful in your overall online marketing efforts.

A good web site is critical to the success of your spa. In order to build a strong company brand, it's simply not enough to have web presence; you need to ensure your web site reflects the image of the business or brand and provides enough information for potential clients. A web site is a great place to educate clients on the types of services offered and the benefits of each service.

Nothing can scare your customers away faster than a poorly designed web site. On the other hand, a properly designed web site can jump-start your business, leading to 99 percent customer retention and attracting new customers on a daily basis. For many potential visitors, their introduction to your spa will be your web site. This is one of the most powerful and cost-effective direct marketing tools you can develop and one that virtually markets itself.

Many inexpensive templates are available through private companies, and a number of free templates are available online. Various web development firms, small marketing and advertising agencies, freelance graphic artists, and copywriters create web sites.

Promote your web site everywhere. Every print ad you run should include your web site. Put your URL on all your business cards, right next to your e-mail address. When embarking on a mailing campaign, direct readers to your web site for more information.

## Steps to Creating a Winning Web Site

A great web site serves as a business center to enhance your career. Different people will visit your site for different reasons at different times. Many factors make the difference between a site that is useless and one that is successful. In fact, putting up a poor web site, one that is out of date and looks like it was designed for a third grade school project is worse than having no site at all. Your site will affect what people will think of your spa business.

- *Web site architecture.* Before you start looking at the visual design, consider what the site is to accomplish. Think about the unique selling proposition of your spa and give that prominence within your site. As you develop an outline, think in terms of the most important and interesting information you want people to have about your business. A web site should be aesthetically appealing, easy to navigate, and informative. It should be an extension of your business, keeping the same color scheme and style of your spa.

- *Visual organization.* The navigational links should be consistent on every page. The home page is the first page the viewer sees. It is critical that it makes a good first impression and does not take forever to download. Photos are excellent visuals for the opening page.

- *Web text.* The writing content of your web site is vital to marketing your spa and should supply the basic information about your business. Use spellcheck but always read the text several times on your own. Many words have double meanings and should always be checked in context.

- *Product and service descriptions.* Provide indepth descriptions about your products and services. Unlike print advertising where you pay by the column inch, web pages offer virtually unlimited space. Use it to gain attention and create interest for your product and service offerings. Treatment pricing and monthly or seasonal specials should be posted on your site, as well as spa packages.

- *Testimonials.* Show off client success stories. Real testimonials will boost your credibility. Ask some of your clients for a short endorsement that you can use on your web site and in other marketing materials. Thank them with an appropriate gift or a discount on their next treatment.

- *Less is more.* Avoid extraneous bells and whistles that can slow users down and prevent them from quickly and easily completing what they came to your site to do. Too many graphics can slow down access.

- *Be consistent.* Keep your navigation bar consistent, prominent on every page, and in the same order so that your clients don't get lost.

- *Contact page.* Put a clear link on the home page that leads to your company's contact information. Include as many forms of communication as you can process, such as telephone and fax numbers, postal mailing address, and e-mail address.

- *FAQs.* Consider using a question-and-answer forum to handle buyer feedback upfront. A *FAQ* section on your web site allows visitors to learn about your products, services, and policies. Anticipate their questions and provide clear, simple answers.

- *Update your web site.* A web site is a constant work in progress. Keep your clients coming back by highlighting spa news on your home page to keep it fresh. Every quarter, if not more frequently, review your site thoroughly to make sure everything is current and all links are still functional. Also, in preparation for marketing for all upcoming holidays, think of ways to accent aspects of your site to make it current. If your site offers special monthly rates on products or services, this will be another reason for visitors to keep coming back.

- *Company policies and guidelines.* Provide as much information to clients about your spa policies as possible before they visit your physical site. Publicize your spa etiquette guidelines on your web site. This will establish boundaries that your business follows when dealing with clients. Spa etiquette also enlightens new spa goers on what is expected and avoided in this relaxing environment.

- *Offer more than just text.* Allow visitors to buy beauty and spa products directly through your site, or include a link to any of the internet mapping sites so that they can easily get driving directions to your facility. Any extras you provide will improve your clients' online experience, which is the first step that leads to their offline experience.

- *Presentation is everything.* As with all web sites, it is critical to present information in a simple, clear, and appealing way. The best sites make it easy for customers to quickly find the information they are looking for.

# Tips for Good Web Writing

Think of a few sites that you like to visit again and again. What makes you keep coming back? Most likely, they offer compelling, relevant, and timely content. Writing for the web is not the same as writing for print. People read differently on the web. They scan read—jumping quickly from one piece of content to the next. People are much more action-oriented on the web. They get online to get something done—and fast. Below are some tips for writing effectively for the web. Use them to take your web site to a higher level.

- *Write relevant content.* It may be tempting to write about your vacation to Hawaii, but if it doesn't relate to your spa site or page topic, leave it out. Web readers want information that is of use to them.

- *Know your reader.* All effective writing begins with knowing your reader. Write for your reader, not for your ego. The most effective writing is keenly focused on the specific needs of a clearly defined reader type. Target your audience through persuasive writing.

- *Keep it evergreen.* "Evergreen" means that the information will not be outdated a month from now. Outdated information can bore your readers. Try to keep your information current as much as possible.

- *Keep your content short and simple.* Get rid of fancy words and jargon. Writing effectively is not about showing off; rather, it is about communicating. Write simply, get to the point, and then stop.

- *Scannable text is vital.* It is important to keep in mind that web surfers don't necessarily always "read" your content. Instead, they scan the page, looking for stand-out words and sentences. This means that in order to attract searchers, you must not only write compelling content, but make it scannable. Long, unbroken blocks of text tend to turn away visitors because they are difficult to read on a computer screen.

  Highlighted text and bulleted lists aid scannability. Use lists instead of paragraphs. Subheadings make the text more scannable. Your readers will move to the section of the document that is most useful for them, and internal cues make it easier for them to do this.

- *Make it easy on your reader.* If searchers can find what they are looking for on your site with a minimum of clicks, then you've got a good chance of having them return. For instance, if your emphasis is tanning, but you choose not to have the word tanning anywhere in your site content, then you are doing a disservice to your readers who are looking for tanning-related information. Quality content must be easy to find and it must be relevant to what the searcher is looking for.

- *Put conclusions at the beginning.* Think of an inverted pyramid when you write. Get to the point in the first paragraph, then expand upon it.

- *Write only one idea per paragraph.* Web pages need to be concise and to the point. People don't *read* web pages, they *scan* them. Having short, meaty paragraphs is better than having long rambling ones.

- *Avoid information overload.* In an average workday, people suffer from information overload. They already have a large volume of e-mails in their inboxes to deal with and therefore may not want to spend time and effort reading content that they do not find useful. Offer your readers information in bite-size chunks that are easily digestible.

- *Take a publishing approach.* Publishing is about getting the right content to the right person at the right time at the right cost. Have timely publishable content that will grab your readers.

- *Write short sentences.* Sentences should be as concise as you can make them. Use only the words you need to get the essential information across.

- *Introduce links.* Links are another way web readers scan pages. They stand out from normal text and provide more cues as to what the page is about.

- *Proofread.* Always, always, always, proofread your work. Typos and spelling errors send people away from your pages. Make sure you proofread everything you post to the web.

- *Target "drive-thru" readers.* Modern society has created drive-thru readers, who are always on the run and have little time to sit and read documents. Readers on the web are impatient. They are in a hurry to get the information they want and move on. They don't have the patience for obscure and complex text, nor do they enjoy scrolling through masses of text either.

  Because there are millions of alternative web sites in cyberspace, readers quickly move to another site if they don't enjoy the information gathering experience on your site.

  Attracting attention and retaining reader interest is a challenge, especially since you have just

  – 10 seconds to grab attention with your web site content.
  – 55 seconds to develop an understanding of your company or product.

  To combat reader fatigue, make it easy for your web users to get relevant information. Put the most important information at the top.

- *Establish trust through your writing content.* Readers on the web are skeptical. Credibility is a major factor in retaining reader interest on the web. To build credibility, use objective language, write meaningful headlines and subheads, and avoid marketing jargon or exaggerated claims.

## Search Engine Submission and Optimization

Search engine submissions are the act of getting your web site listed with search engines. Another term for this is *search engine registration*. Make sure you have the right keywords. Getting listed within search engines does not mean that you will necessarily rank well for particular terms. It simply means that the search engine knows your pages exist. For example, if your signature treatments are seaweed body wraps and sunless tanning, then include these descriptions with your submissions.

Web site directories are search engines powered by human beings. Human editors compile all the listings that directories have. Getting listed with the web's key directories is very important because these listings are seen by many people. In addition, if

---

# Web Site Dos and Don'ts

## Do

- ○ Make it clear what you do and what you are offering on the homepage.
- ○ Give your full postal address, to establish credibility.
- ○ Provide an opportunity for feedback by e-mail, telephone, or regular mail.
- ○ Include some background information on your business.
- ○ Offer added value on the site, with useful information and free downloads.
- ○ Have a "return to home" button on each page.
- ○ Make your site easy to follow and user friendly.
- ○ Keep the site information current and display the date that you last modified the page contents.
- ○ Keep the number and size of graphics on your site to a minimum as graphics download slowly from the Internet.

## Don't

- ○ Include too many photos on your opening page, as they tend to slow down the access.
- ○ Have too many layers requiring a great deal of mouse clicking.
- ○ Insist on registration simply to get on your site.
- ○ Be anonymous; provide contact names and e mail addresses.
- ○ Ever forget that the site is a sales tool first and not someplace to show "cool" stuff that does not contribute to your sales and advertising goals.

---

you are listed with them, then crawler-based search engines are more likely to find your site and add it to their listings for free.

The key to good search engine placement is content. The more information that you offer on your subject, the more likely your web page will achieve a high ranking. Many search engines examine the content of a page to see if it is really related to the targeted keywords. They also measure word count.

Search engines have a hard time indexing web sites that are in frames or that have a Flash introduction. Keep your front page simple with content that is relevant. This will give you a better chance of rising in the rankings.

# 8

# Marketing Tips for Spa Owners

The reality of every spa owner is this: you *are* your business. It is up to you to market your spa services in order to benefit from your talent, hard work, and dedication.

Pursuing the right marketing strategies is critical to your financial success. Presentation is everything when it comes to marketing materials. Whether you are developing a brochure, an ad, or a newsletter, your marketing collateral sends a strong message about your spa. Materials should be well written, attractive, and professional.

The ideas discussed in this chapter can be part of your marketing plan. Not all of them will work for your spa. Select the ones that suit your specific needs. They are intended to help you establish visibility and credibility, and to enhance marketability.

Most ideas costs less than $100 to put into effect, but bear in mind that the same service can cost you over $1,000 if you want to go high end. Some tips don't even cost you a penny; they require time, energy, and a positive attitude. Remember, marketing efforts need to be followed systematically and consistently over a period of time. Don't expect overnight results.

The marketing strategies are categorized under: (1) writing-related marketing efforts; (2) volunteer-based marketing strategies; (3) gift marketing; (4) advertising; and (5) word-of-mouth marketing.

# Writing-Related Marketing Efforts

The written word is always a great way to let people know what you are doing. There are a number of choices for your platform. The following will give you some good ideas on how to get started.

## Newsletters

Start a newsletter to promote your spa. Newsletters are one of the least expensive and most effective public relations tools for drawing attention to your spa. This is especially true with e-newsletters. By sending out a quality newsletter on a regular basis, you can keep current clients, potential clients, the media, and other important sources updated about your business.

Some questions to answer in your newsletter are:

- What's unique about your spa?
- Who are your clients? This tells you what kind of audience you are writing to.
- What services are you proudest of? Describe them briefly.
- Have you won any spa-related awards?
- Are there any clients who would provide testimonials about your services?

In addition, you should also:

- Allow room for photographs.
- Encourage readers to send you e-mail.
- Include a "Safe Unsubscribe" feature.
- Provide a list of URLs where readers can find out more information.

- Include a headline for every article and a caption for every picture.
- Double-check your spelling and grammar. If you are weak in these areas, have someone else read the newsletter with an editor's eye before e-mailing it.
- Cultivate a mailing list. Keep it in good shape and work on expanding it. The more people see your newsletter the more business you are likely to get.

## "We've Missed You" Postcards

Remember how the dentist's office sends you reminders every six months to get your teeth cleaned? Usually it works. The secretary follows up with a call, reminding you that getting your teeth cleaned prevents cavities. Follow the same tactic with your spa business. Send a postcard to those customers who haven't visited your spa in three months. Tell them that they have been missed and that you would like to see them again. Address cards to a specific name, and not "To whom it may concern."

A postcard has an immediate impact on readers. They don't have to open an envelope. On one side include an image or two of your spa services. Give a bold heading with your spa name. On the other side write a brief one to two line description of your work and include some pricing of specific services. Don't overcrowd the postcard with too many photos or too much writing. Leave plenty of blank space to soothe the eye. Best of all, postcards are a useful and inexpensive method of print advertising.

## Press Releases

You can write a press release about nearly anything newsworthy that is related to your spa. Some topics include a new facial that you are introducing, an open house, or the display of new medical spa technology. Some magazines, newspapers, and public radio stations promote press releases for free. Do a little bit of legwork to find out if there are any sources that promote press releases at no charge in your area.

### Smart Tip

Tip...

Some tips for writing press releases:

- Submit the press release well before the publishing deadline.
- Keep the press release short.
- Follow the guidelines.
- Write to catch the eye and hold the reader's interest.
- Include a good photograph or two with the press release.

## Subscribe to Spa Magazines

Subscribing to spa magazines helps you to keep in touch with the latest trends in the spa industry. There are so many magazines to choose from. Select the ones that will be the most valuable to you. The presence of current spa magazines on your business premises also helps to enhance your image. This lets customers know that you are in touch with the latest trends in the industry.

# Apply for Grants

Private foundation, corporations, nonprofit organizations, and community foundations award grants for spa-related activities. The majority of grants are given to organizations with nonprofit status. You may increase your chance of winning grants by affiliating with a nonprofit organization.

Usually an organization seeks support in one or more of the following categories:

- *Operating (general) support*. Funds for operations are used to cover the costs of running programs that meet community needs.
- *Capital/equipment*. Funds for remodeling and renovation, additional buildings, construction, building expansion, and the purchase of land or equipment.
- *Special projects*. Funds for special projects are monies restricted by the funder to starting a new program within a limited time.

# Promote Your Web Site Every Day

Be sure your web site is featured on your business cards, reception area, brochures, and all other business-related paraphernalia. The more easily customers can find your web address, the more likely they are to visit your site. Offline marketing is as important as online marketing.

# Contact Local Writers to Promote your Spa

Get travel writers interested in your spa. If you treat them well and they like you, their reviews can be a hundred times more effective than an ad in a glossy spa magazine. Magazine and newspaper editors are constantly looking for fresh ideas, both in writing and photography. You can increase business by getting a feature article published in a newspaper or trade magazine. Getting your spa into a spa trade journal is a sure way to market your services. The key is to enlighten readers about your spa and how you can improve their quality of life.

# Flying High

A flier is a standard 8.5-inch-by-11-inch letter-size sheet of paper that can be used to create awareness, present information, and promote your spa services. Fliers have a local reach. You can often work with a flier-distribution company or the post office to target a very specific neighborhood or area. The cost of fliers can be very low if you focus on a particular area.

# Volunteer-Based Marketing Strategies

Creating goodwill by volunteering your services is always a savvy marketing plan.

## Pro Bono Work

Pro bono work is particularly effective when you want to promote your spa in a new area or when your business needs a refreshingly new burst. Offer services to homeless shelters, welfare organizations, hospice centers, and community schools. Pro bono work does not necessarily have to be related to your spa services; it can be anything that helps to increase your visibility in the community.

Charitable work always reflects well on your business. It shows that you venture beyond yourself. Community involvement shows people that you take a genuine interest in their well-being outside your business parameters. It provides your spa with more exposure, which increases client loyalty and sales. Some examples of pro bono work are:

- Donating complimentary skin treatments/make-up sessions for actresses participating in a community film festival
- Sponsoring a fundraiser organized by a local nonprofit
- Displaying a local photographer's artwork in your salon for a limited time.
- Offering free hair cutting sessions at the local nursing home for elderly residents. All these are ways of showing community involvement.

## Philanthropic Activities

Giving is not just good for the soul, but is also good for business. Often, when donating services for a charity event, a logo or ad is included in the program or on the organization's web site.

# Gift Marketing

There are many ways to take advantage of this marketing element. You can even mix and match ideas to best suit your business.

## Gift Certificates

Give gift certificates to your customers as holiday gifts. Typically, gift certificates are nonrefundable. They should be transferable to another person. Gift certificates can be purchased pre-formatted and blank, from office supply stores.

# Gift with Purchase (GWP)

This is a brilliant marketing strategy—everybody loves to get a present. It is a great incentive both for the business and the client. Clients often extend their budgets to hit the target amount needed to obtain the GWP, and the GWP provides a product to sample and then to fall in love with. Some vendors offer programs to assist you with contributing the GWP. It should be associated with a special event or be available only for a specific duration. It never should extend over a long period of time, or the excitement will be lost. A "while supplies last" type of promotion usually works very well.

# Gratis

Gratis is the practice of receiving a retail product at no charge. There are copious ways of using this technique. Create thank-you gifts out of the free samples that you get. Hand them out to each customer in a particular week. Be sure that you have a "sales pitch" to go along with the product. Announce the free samples in your newsletter. For example, "All customers getting treatments at *Serene Spa* during the week of October 5th to October 12th will receive free aloe vera lotion." This will be an incentive for customers to purposely schedule their appointments during that specific week. You should try out a strategy like this during a slow season, not during a peak holiday week like Christmas.

# Gift Card Strategies

An aggressive gifting strategy is vital to your spa and salon business. Plastic electronic gift cards are becoming popular and trendy. The credit-card-sized gift card has an intoxicating consumer appeal. They are stylish, small, and a welcome gift, especially at holiday time. When a guest exhausts the credit card balance, it can be recharged on the same card.

# Raffle Prizes

Hold a raffle. Select a particular week to hand out a raffle ticket to every customer who walks into your spa. At the end of the week, select a winner and award a prize. Raffle tickets are inexpensive and can be purchased at party supply stores. This makes your spa a fun place to visit and creates an incentive for your clients to keep coming back.

# Advertising

Naturally, traditional forms of advertising will help get your business known. The following are some suggestions you may not have thought of.

## Cooperative Advertising

This offers marketing support for you and a specific product line and is processed in different ways, depending on the supplier. Most manufacturers or suppliers designate an allotted dollar amount to go toward co-op advertising. The spa owner creates an advertisement you send it to the supplier for approval featuring that product and the spa, so it can be sure you present the brand properly. Once the ad is approved, it is placed. The product company credits the spa's account for the percentage it is reimbursing, which can be used for future purchases.

## Yellow Page Ads

Yellow Pages are a powerful way to acquire new customers. Hair and beauty salons are one of the top ten categories people look for in their Yellow Pages.

## Print Ads

Print ads are one of the most powerful and popular methods of advertising. Consistency is one of the most important elements of successful advertising. Keep the same image and layout throughout your ad campaign. When advertising in a local magazine or newspaper, keep the logo and photo the same in each ad. Even when the text changes, your ad layout still will be familiar to consumers, thereby helping to build your brand. An advertisement should be easy to read, easy to understand, and stand out while readers flip through a publication.

## Business Card

Your business card can become a powerful tool for promotion. Ideally, it should include your name, company name, address, web site, phone, and fax. Think of your business card as a mini advertisement. Your aim is to get people who read it to call or visit you. Create custom, full-color designs that will creatively connect you with your target market while visually building your image. Use quality paper, make it easy to read, and keep it simple.

Despite the availability of expensive designs and die cuts, the most recommended form is a standard size business card that fits neatly into a wallet, card case, or Rolodex®. What is important is that you include all of the basic information about your business such as the name, street address, telephone number, e-mail, web site, and, when necessary, title/name of employee. Leave enough white space and don't clutter your card with too much information.

## Spa Stationery

Elegant stationery is a great way to polish your presentation. Letterhead, note cards, envelopes, reminder cards, gift cards, and referral cards can improve the quality of your spa's image tremendously.

# Word-of-Mouth Marketing

Nothing can replace goodwill and word-of-mouth referrals. No good deed goes unnoticed, so make yourself visible to your community.

## Cultivate Referrals

People invariably listen to a personal recommendation over a sales pitch. Word of mouth is a strong means of promoting your spa. Referrals are also among the most profitable means of marketing. A referral from a present customer is stronger than an ad in the local paper.

In order to get quality referrals, it is important to have ongoing, frequent contact with your clients. Simply ask your present customers for a referral. An option that will cost you as little as $5 is to have business cards printed that say "Refer a Friend." Have a space for your customer to write his/her name. This is a great way to find out who your most valued customers are as well. For every new client that comes to you via a referral, offer the customer that referred her a discount or thank-you gift.

## Building Bridges not Boundaries

Building relationships with other local businesses is an excellent way to increase visibility. Giving gift certificates to the right people is an affordable way to promote business. Join your local chamber of commerce, Rotary, or church council. Collaborate with your competitors, instead of avoiding them. All these are ways of building bridges instead of boundaries—locally, nationally, and internationally.

# Spa
# Ambience

A hand carved marble piece of Lotus sculpture lit with a soft red light strengthens a couple's love for one another; a spa guest enjoys the soothing music of Beethoven's *Pastorale Symphony*; a young mother enjoys a delicious seafood dish.

All these are examples of spa ambience—the atmosphere that you create in a way that is appealing to guests. Spa ambience that connects cuisine, music, lighting, and sculpture makes guests feel special and gives a touch of finesse to their experience at your spa. It can elevate the quality of your spa service from ordinary to extraordinary.

To ensure an overall superior spa ambience and client satisfaction, begin by surveying the spa experience as a client does—from entering the spa to the checkout process. What truly sets your spa apart from others is the overall experience clients enjoy when visiting. As the owner, you must be able to identify areas that require special attention and improvement from the moment a client enters your spa to the moment she leaves your premises. In the ideal spa experience, details make all the difference. Playing to your clients' different senses can enhance their experience and your business. Successful spas are reaping benefits because of their focus on accommodating all of the senses for a complete experience.

Some of the components of spa ambience are:

1. *Gustatory impact.* Greet your guests with a welcoming drink that sets the right taste in their mouths. Include a complimentary snack in individual rooms. Make your spa menu appeal to different palates.

2. *Auditory impact.* Music should enhance the atmosphere rather than disrupt or overwhelm. Choose your music wisely and select it for its calming and serene qualities. Introduce music not only in the reception area but also in the dining section, pool, garden, treatment rooms, bathrooms, and meditation areas.

3. *Visual impact.* From the image of the spa to the overall disposition of team members, the visual impact that clients experience is a key factor in the overall success of your spa. The right choice of paintings, sculpture, plants, furniture, accessories, ornaments, carpeting, tapestry, and accents project a message of relaxation, comfort, and wellness.

4. *Aromatic (olfactory) impact.* Make sure that when a client first arrives the scent of your spa sets the mood for the overall wellness experience. Use candles and incense to invite the client into the spa. Just remember not to overwhelm your clients with too powerful a fragrance.

# Spa Cuisine

Pan-seared cod with baby spinach and steamed mushrooms. Sounds like an exotic gourmet dish, right? It's actually spa cuisine, a trend that has evolved to become some of the best food in the hospitality industry.

So, what exactly is spa cuisine? Although the term is somewhat nebulous, spa cuisine refers to a return to the simpler and less refined ways of the past in preparing and cooking food. The focus is on natural ingredients and simple cooking with an emphasis on presentation. It is a nutritious approach that promotes healthy eating—a balance of whole grains, fresh fruit, vegetables, dairy products, and lean protein.

Spa cuisine is an important part of the destination spa agenda where guests stay for long periods. "Healthy but boring" is a common slogan associated with good food. Spa cuisine, however, steps beyond this image and makes it interesting. What your guests eat can make or break your spa business. Your guests seek something bold, flavorful, and satisfying to safeguard their health and to enjoy eating at your spa. The food they eat needs to transport your guests back to basics and complement the treatments offered at your spa. Instead of separating it from the rest of your spa operations, carefully integrate spa cuisine into your marketing plan.

The three C's of spa cuisine are color, contrast, and crunch. Bright colors indicate good nutritional value, and obviously, they make the food look appealing. Food should have contrast in terms of color, texture, flavor, and temperature. Freshness is key, with produce from local farms emphasized. Crunchy vegetables are freshly picked, and sometimes served raw. Vegetable stocks and acidic-based marinades with less oil and fat take the front seat in spa cuisine. Examples of spa cuisine include grains, fresh vegetables and fruit, free range poultry, brightly colored fresh fruit and vegetables, lean dairy or calcium-rich nondairy sources, grains, legumes, beans, clean water, and lean protein sources.

# Ten Key Components of Spa Cuisine

1. Utilizes preparation and cooking methods that maximize and enhance flavor, texture, and nutrition.
2. Limits sugar and artificial sweeteners, with minimal saturated trans fats.
3. Promotes optimal health and well-being.
4. Emphasizes organic, vegetarian foods and eco-cuisine.
5. Provides pleasurable and satisfying sensations.
6. Uses natural and innovative substitutes to create healthier food options.
7. Emphasizes mindful portion sizes in every meal.
8. Incorporates and promotes the sustainability of agricultural resources; fresh food is key.
9. Features seasonally fresh foods with high nutritional value and minimal processing.
10. Fulfills individual nutritional needs and preferences.

▲

Attention to presentation is key in spa cuisine. Chefs go the extra mile to present their dishes in aesthetically arresting ways.

Another essential quality is to include food with supreme medicinal value. Herbs come to the forefront. Their proper usage requires chefs to know the finer points of medicinal properties and appearance, not just flavor. For example ginger doesn't just perk up the taste buds, it also aids digestion and adds a pleasant aroma; lemongrass lends more to a meal than just its citrus tang as it also clears one's breathing tracts.

# Spa Music

A Lomi Lomi massage to the sound of the waves of the Polynesian sea; sitar music playing an Indian Raga to a soothing Shirodhara head massage; a Rachmaninoff Symphony during a Swedish massage. Spa music has become a necessary ingredient in day, medical, destination, and spiritual spas throughout the country. Spa professionals have found that relaxing to the sound of music produces long lasting healing effects on their clients physically, emotionally, and spiritually. What's more, spa music is becoming a powerful marketing tool that helps to draw more clients. It can be carefully integrated into your service menu as a marketing device. Music supports the sale of an overall image.

Music is energy, and proper energy is a fundamental key to a successful spa operation. To truly appeal to clients in this context and create incremental profits, select music that integrates naturally with the spa environment.

---

## Incorporating Music into Your Spa Menu

❍ The quiet sounds of ragas can soothe a client receiving an Indian head massage.

❍ The sound of waves gently crashing against rocks can lull a client into a deep slumber at night.

❍ The right music can put customers into the right mood to buy skin care products. Music can be a deciding factor that determines whether or not customers buy products and services.

❍ The correct choice of music during meals can enhance the pleasure associated with eating.

❍ The yoga and meditation center is ideal for a musical lifestyle. Introduce soft and soothing music to these areas where clients come to relax.

❍ The right choice of music can evoke and create a sense of balance in the body, mind, and spirit of spa guests.

---

One of the first things opportunities spas have to help their clients prepare for and fully accept the treatments they receive is to provide music that is conducive to relaxation and peace. Spa music is the kind of music that brings to listeners the feeling of peace and relaxation. This also means that spa music is conductive to the mind so it helps us get better results from other body practices.

# How to Introduce the Sound of Music

Follow a series of steps when introducing the sound of music to spa guests. Firstly, select the appropriate music. Choose calming and soothing music to relax your clients. Sometimes it is necessary to first choose music that matches your client's current mood rather than the mood the he or she wants to acquire. This is known as sequencing music. Arrange a series of different musical compositions in sequence, customized for client's needs. For example, if you are dealing with depression, select a composition that represents feelings of melancholy such as soft flute music. End the session with a composition that is uplifting and motivating. Listening to music in a sequence like this allows current stress levels or moods to be first honored and then to be gradually transformed.

Spa clients need to learn the art of relaxing to music. Preparing your clients for the musical environment is important. Start with low volume and do not interrupt the music listening process with conversation. Create a calm environment for the guest.

# Therapeutic Qualities of Music

- Music captivates and maintains attention, stimulating and utilizing many parts of the brain.
- Music is an effective memory aid.
- Music supports and encourages movement.
- Music and its related silence provide nonverbal, immediate feedback.
- Music sets up a social context by setting up a safe, structured setting for verbal and nonverbal communication.
- Music transforms pain into relaxation.
- Music structures time in a way that we can understand.

Speakers help to enhance the quality of the sound. Speakers can revitalize the way your clients hear music. Clients can listen to music through speakers rather than headphones so that the cells of the body themselves may "listen" to the sound.

# Spa Lighting

A honeymoon couple sits by the pool, surrounded by soft red fiber optic lighting illuminating the water; spa guests are surrounded by bright fluorescent lights in the dining area; a couple strolling through the garden enjoys the lighting illuminating the trees and bushes around the spa premises. Imagine an environment that will dazzle and amaze your spa visitors. These aesthetic delights make a difference and can help to draw more clients to your spa. Lighting can make or break a client's experience at your spa.

Enhance the intimacy of your spa environment with the correct choice of lighting. Introducing proper lighting techniques can truly enhance the intimate and warm atmosphere of your spa. The current market offers a wide variety of lighting products ranging from bright fluorescent to rice paper lanterns. Carefully select the correct lighting to make your spa a pleasant experience for your guests.

Lighting is an important component design that serves two main purposes: enhancing the ambience and helping functionality in supporting operations. Natural lighting can be used to your advantage, thereby saving energy during the day. Solariums, glass windows, sky roofing, verandahs, and patios are ways to capture natural lighting.

In treatment areas, lighting should support the task at hand. Dimmer switches, soft accent lights, and candles work well in treatment rooms. In such areas lighting is an important part of setting the mood for a relaxing massage. External lighting of your pool, spa, or water feature is possible with a variety of high- and low-voltage systems. Use correct lighting to light up your portable Jacuzzi, whirlpool, and hot tub. Lighting can transform your daytime pool or spa into a paradise of nighttime color and beauty. Adding light to any pool or spa increases safety, promotes use after dark, and creates excitement.

Fiber optic lighting has become a popular form of spa lighting. Illuminate a fountain or waterfall from within; or create a moving palette of color by synchronizing all your water features. Fiber optics provide a soothing feel for your swimming pool. The illuminator or light source contains a spinning color wheel that is distributed through the fiber optic cable and out of the light fixture. The possibilities are endless when the night is alive with color and brilliance.

Guests can press of a button, and the computer-generated digital lighting allows them to select a rotation of changing color or a permanent display of their favorite tone, accompanied by a soothing choice of music. Some lights allow guests to adjust the various colored lenses to suit the mood and ambience in individual rooms. Introducing the correct lighting into individual guest rooms can enable guests to enjoy the radiance of soft color.

# Spa Sculpture *Does* Make a Difference

A widow strolls across a Zen rock garden, calming her anxieties about the recent loss of her husband; a couple enjoys a dinner by a Renaissance-style marble fireplace; a group of teenagers enjoy outdoor massages in a bamboo environment. Choosing the right sculpture can enhance the warm and friendly atmosphere of your spa, thereby attracting more customers. Sculpture must be carefully selected to suit your spa layout as it helps to accentuate the spa theme. In most spas, an interior designer is responsible for the indoor decorating, and a landscape architect is responsible for the outdoors.

Introducing the right sculpture into the massage rooms can set the tone and mood for treatments. For an outdoor massage room defined along a tropical theme, bamboo sculpture can yield an earthy and eco-friendly feel. A massage bed, ornaments, and roof made with bamboo will add a touch of elegance to your spa. Buddha statues are a popular item in Ayurveda spas, yoga retreats, eco-friendly spas, and meditation centers.

## Ideas for Spa Sculpture

Choosing the right sculpture for your spa can make a tremendous difference in the way guests feel when they enter your establishment. Here are some ideas for spa sculpture.

### BIRD BATHS

Bird baths are popular items, especially in tropical spas. Stone bird baths with intricate carvings are becoming popular again. The presence of birds creates a soothing effect and is always a pleasant welcome to spa guests.

### BIRD FEEDERS

Wooden bird feeders hung outside individual guest rooms are delightful additions. Guests get immense pleasure from watching birds feed, especially during wintertime. It contributes to the overall sense of well-being exuded by your spa environment. The sight of birds in the vicinity of your spa reinforces the balance between people and animals.

## CARVED ANIMALS

Carved animals such as frogs, birds, dolphins, and horses adorn spa gardens and interiors. They help to create an earthy atmosphere and reinforce the connection between man and nature. Carved animals are especially popular in theme-specific spas such as rainforest spas and green spas.

## ARCHITECTURAL ORNAMENTS

Gothic architecture is a frequent source of ornaments in spas. Gothic architectural steps, balconies, trellises, arches, gates, and roofing enhance the indoor and outdoor appearance of European-style spas.

## CUSTOM SIGNAGE

Carved signage gives identity and image to your spa. Hire a professional engraver to design your outdoor signage.

## SCULPTURE GARDENS

A Buddha garden is a common motif in Ayurveda spas. Some have themes of the Hindu god Ganesh or Shiva to decorate their spa gardens. Other oriental-style Zen spas have outdoor walking meditation gardens and Zen rock gardens that are simply but tastefully decorated with sculpture.

## PONDS AND INDOOR WATERFALLS

Fish ponds and indoor waterfalls are soothing to the eye and are especially welcoming in medical spas. Spa visitors love to seek quietude in these settings. Hire a sculptor or carver to decorate your aqua environment with images of dolphins, frogs, and coral. Some of these faux finishes can give an elegant feel to your spa.

## WATER FOUNTAINS FOR THE OUTDOOR POND/LAKE

A fountain gives life to a pond/lake. Fountains with water gushing from a lion's mouth have made a comeback in modern resort and medical spas.

## CARVED FIREPLACES FOR THE INDOORS

Hand-carved fireplaces in limestone and marble can make beautiful additions, especially in spas with Victorian architecture. Fireplaces can be carved from Baroque to modern styles. Log online to find out about places selling hand-carved fireplaces for the indoors.

## POOL SCULPTURE

The right choice of gates, fences, and trellises can enhance your pool area. In addition, carved animals, carved benches, and lamp posts can decorate the outdoor pool area.

## FUNCTIONAL SCULPTURE

Introducing functional sculpture is a current and trendy way of giving a touch of finesse to your spa services. Sculptors use recycled metal, car parts, plastic, and ceramic to make astounding works of functional sculpture. Pieces range from candle holders, through steel fireplace screens, to mugs, plates, and kitchenware.

# 10

# Sensual
# Healing

**M**assage is the practice of applying structured or unstructured pressure, tension, motion, or vibration to the soft tissues of the body to achieve a beneficial response. A form of therapy, massage can be applied to parts of the body or successively to the whole body, to aid the process of injury healing, relieve psychological stress, manage pain, and improve circulation.

# Massage Basics

Massage is the application of touch by one person to another using manual techniques of rubbing, stroking, kneading, and compression. The word *massage* is believed to have derived from the Arabic word *masah*, which means to stroke with the hand or press softly. Massage can alleviate physical, mental, and emotional ailments and is central to the modern spa industry.

# Massage Through the Ages

Although massage has probably existed in rudimentary form for as long as humans have, most believe that the Chinese were the first to systemize it. As early as 3000 B.C., the Chinese used a combination of herbs, exercise, and massage on the body in a type of massage known as *amma*. Ancient Egyptian drawings from as early as 2500 B.C. show medical practitioners treating the hands and feet of patients. These drawings are considered by many to represent an early form of massage called reflexology. Massage has been well known in India for over 3,000 years in the ancient medical system of Ayurveda. The Japanese further developed massage to manipulate chi, or the life force, within the body. They also developed a method of finger pressure on particular points of the body called shiatsu.

Remember what Hippocrates, the father of modern medicine, said about massage, "A physician must be experienced in many things," he wrote, "but assuredly in rubbing, for rubbing can bind a joint that is too loose, and loosen a joint that is too rigid." The Roman emperor's physician Galen (A.D. 199) wrote at least 16 books relating to massage and exercise. He classified massage into firm, gentle, and moderate. It is said that Julius Caesar was given a daily massage. The Romans developed the art of massage, using it as an integral part of hygiene and as a medical treatment for many conditions.

# Massage Today

Massage today is in many ways a return to what our ancestors introduced to us thousands of years ago. After five thousand years, we are only beginning to uncover massage's dramatic benefits, its physical, mental, emotional, and social effects. Massage is the perfect personal and physiological therapy for the 21st century.

As we move into a new era, people all over the world are becoming increasingly aware of the importance of integrating body, mind, and soul for the ultimate satisfaction of total fitness and good health. The 21st century promises a new kind of self and social consciousness where body and mind care are supreme for the self and a vital link to connecting with fellow beings. Massage is the perfect system for such a mode of living. Massage helps to connect with our inner selves and outer environments naturally and wholly.

Massage is now being used in ICUs for children, elderly people, babies in incubators, and patients with cancer, AIDS, heart attacks, and strokes. Most American hospices have some kind of bodywork therapy available, and it is frequently offered in health centers, drug treatment clinics, and pain clinics. Nursing homes are required to have occupational therapists attending to their residents.

# Basic Massage Techniques

There are many massage techniques, and finding the best technique is usually a matter of personal preference and type of treatment being offered. Common massage techniques include:

- *Stroking.* The rhythmic flowing movements of stroking form the basis of massage.
- *Kneading.* This movement is useful on the shoulders and fleshy areas such as the hips and thighs. It stretches and relaxes tense muscles and improves the circulation, bringing fresh blood and nutrients to the area.

## Benefits of Massage

**M**assage is a powerful healing touch that results in increased physical and mental health for both the receiver and the giver. Massage

- ○ relieves stress, tension, fatigue, and anxiety.
- ○ increases the oxygen-carrying capacity of the blood.
- ○ loosens contracted muscles.
- ○ stimulates sluggish muscles.
- ○ balances the nervous system.
- ○ helps break up and facilitates elimination of the waste products or harmful toxins that build up in overworked muscle tissue.
- ○ improves circulation to internal organs.
- ○ improves circulation to the skin.
- ○ helps the body to release endorphins (chemicals that relieve pain).

- *Pressures.* Deep, direct pressure is extremely useful for releasing tension in the muscles, either side of the spine, and around the shoulders.
- *Percussion.* Brisky, bouncy percussion movements are useful on fleshy, muscular areas.
- *Knuckling.* Knuckling is commonly used on the shoulders, chest, palms of the hand, and soles of the feet for a rippling effect.

# Massage Surroundings

The massage environment should be airy, spacious, hygienic, and welcoming. It needs to give an impression of order, calmness, and efficiency. Temperatures should be kept around 70 degrees Fahrenheit. Soft, suffused lighting is advisable, and direct rays should never be on the face. A musical background is favored by many practitioners while others opt for silence.

Clients must be encouraged to ask as many questions as they want before treatments. This can save massage therapists the hassle of being asked questions by a client during a treatment.

### HOW OFTEN SHOULD CLIENTS GET A MASSAGE?

There is no hard and fast rule on this. Clients can receive massages as often or as infrequently as they like.

### SHOULD CLIENTS EAT BEFORE A MASSAGE?

It is best not to eat immediately preceding or proceeding a massage. Refined sugars, high fats, caffeine, and alcohol must be avoided for one hour before and after the massage. These can have a stronger effect on the clients than normal. Because bodywork introduces clean, oxygenated, and nourished fluids into the tissues and stimulates the body to purge toxins, it is important to flush them out by drinking plenty of water.

### SHOULD CLIENTS BE NUDE FOR A MASSAGE?

The best way to receive a massage is unclothed. However, American spas never require their clients to be naked if it makes them uncomfortable. Train your spa therapists in the "art of draping." This makes spa clients less self-conscious as they are covered with a sheet at all times, and only the part being massaged is exposed.

### WHAT SHOULD CLIENTS DO BEFORE A MASSAGE?

Encourage clients to wear loose, comfortable clothing and to remove jewelry. To enhance the relaxation process, schedule a time of day when they have a few hours to rest both before and after the massage. Showering before a massage needs to be recommended. If some clients prefer to take a dip in the pool, they should shower briefly before jumping into the swimming pool. If clients use the sauna or steam bath, they need to always sit on their towels and wear the plastic shoes provided by the spa.

## WHAT SHOULD CLIENTS DO AFTER A MASSAGE TREATMENT?

Some clients may not know post-massage etiquette. As the spa owner, it is your responsibility to educate them about what they can do to get the most out of their massage experience. Encourage them to take a few minutes to enjoy the moment. Ask them to stretch, take a few deep breaths, and stabilize before getting up. They need to avoid consuming alcohol immediately after the treatment. If clients are transitioning to another treatment, a member of the staff needs to be trained to direct clients to the next session.

## WHEN SHOULD CLIENTS REFRAIN FROM GETTING A MASSAGE?

Educate your clients about when they should avoid massage treatments. If they have conditions such as herpes, open wounds or sores, healing incisions, and infectious diseases, massage should be avoided. Make it mandatory in your health questionnaire to find out if your clients are epileptic or pregnant. Never give a massage if a client has a high fever. Most spas refuse to give massages to visibly intoxicated guests.

# Aromatherapy: It Makes Scents

"Aroma" derives from the Greek word for spice. "Aromatherapy" means "treatment using scents." It refers to the use of essential oils in holistic healing to improve one's health and emotional well-being and to restore balance in the body. Fragrant essential oils can enrich one's life, whether they are used therapeutically, in beauty treatments, to perfume a spa, or for sheer pleasure.

When oils are combined with massage, their effectiveness in relieving stress, improving mood, and promoting good health is most striking. Massage with aromatic oils softens the skin and aids healing. Numerous powers have been attributed to fragrant plants. They have been used throughout history in the pursuit of happiness and health, as part of medicine, religion, magic, and cosmetics. In early civilizations, scented woods and oils were often burned to communicate with Gods or to exorcise demons. Even today incense is part of healing ceremonies in many cultures.

Aromatherapy massage is an art that involves an intimate interaction between the person giving the massage, the person receiving it, and the aroma of the oils. When you offer aromatherapy massages to your clients, personalize each blend to give the effect your client desires. This can go a long way from a marketing point of view. Pamper your clients with aromatic beauty treatments, and they will return for more.

# Essential Oils

Here are some essential oils of aromatherapy that you can introduce to your spa:

- *Bergamot (Citrus bergamia).* Widely used in Italian folk medicine, bergamot gets its name from an Italian village. The oil helps to allay depression, heal wounds, and soothe skin problems.

- *Chamomile (Chamaemelum nobile/ Matricaria recutita).* Chamomile has a soothing effect and is well suited to treating children. It eases anxiety, insomnia, stress-related headaches, and premenstrual tension.

- *Cypress (Cupressus sempervirens).* In many cultures, the cypress tree represents eternal life. Plato (c. 429–47 B.C.) referred to it as the symbol of immortality. Cypress oil is used to treat respiratory complaints and in foot massages.

- *Eucalyptus (Eucalyptus globules).* Traditionally, Australian Aboriginal people bound the leaves of the indigenous Eucalyptus tree to wounds to speed healing. The main constituent, cineol, is responsible for its powerful antiseptic, antiviral, and expectorant effects. It is used in chest massage.

- *Frankincense (Boswellia carterii/Boswellia thurifera).* A chest massage with frankincense can deepen breathing. It has a divine fragrance.

- *Geranium (Pelargonium graveolens).* Traditionally, geranium was used to stanch bleeding, and heal wounds and ulcers. Geranium is good for acne treatments because of its antimicrobial effect.

- *Jasmine (Jasminum grandiflorum).* Exquisitely fragranced, jasmine is reputed to be an aphrodisiac. The flowers of the jasmine plant, cultivated in India and North Africa, yield tiny amounts of oil. In Ayurvedic medicine, jasmine is recommended for cleansing the blood. Jasmine is also used as an anti-depressant and to treat lethargy.

- *Juniper (Juniperus communis).* Its antiviral properties make juniper useful in treating respiratory infections and it is an ideal air freshener. Juniper is often used in anticellulite massage blends.

- *Lavender (Lavandula angustifolia).* In 1910 Renee Maurice Gattefosse, a French perfumerist and chemist, accidentally rinsed his hands in Lavender essence, thereby halting the onset of gangrene that had developed from a burn. His swift and successful recovery was a catalyst for research into the properties of essential oils. Lavender is an antiseptic and is used to treat acne and eczema. It is also used in herbal pillows.

- *Lemongrass (Cymbopogon citrates)*. Lemongrass has many pain-relieving properties. It also acts as a digestive tonic, diuretic, and antiseptic. In India it is widely used in Ayurvedic medicine to treat fevers and infections. It acts as a sedative on the central nervous system.

- *Marjoram (Origanum majorana)*. Marjoram was reputedly created by Aphrodite, the Greek goddess of love, as a symbol of happiness and well-being. Massages with marjoram ease aches.

- *Peppermint (Mentha piperita)*. Grows in abundance in Morocco, where it is served as a delicious tea. Peppermint oil is also an excellent mental stimulant and digestive aid.

- *Rose (Rosa centifolia/Rosa damascena)*. Roses have long been associated with Venus, Roman goddess of love and beauty. Rose oil is used in facial massages and skin products.

- *Sandalwood (Santalum album)*. Mentioned in the *Nirkuta*, the oldest of the Hindu *Vedas* (written in the 5th century B.C.), sandalwood was used in religious ceremonies in India. It is used in Indian Ayurvedic medicine. Sandalwood is used to calm and cool the body and to reduce inflammation, infection, and fever. It is popular in beauty products.

- *Tea tree (Melaleuca alternifolia)*. The Australian Aboriginal people used poultices of the leaves on wounds and cuts and smoked the leaves to clear congestion. Tea tree oil is ideal for the feet.

# Exotic Spa Ideas from the
## Orient

More and more spas have begun to introduce oriental themes into their spa agendas. Blending oriental ideas into a nonoriental landscape can give a refreshing outlook and intimate elegance to your spa. Feng shui, Ayurveda, and Zen are just a handful of spa themes that trace their origins to the oriental world.

Start Your Own Day Spa and More

Below are some exotic spa ideas from the orient. They have been borrowed from spas found in Indonesia, Sri Lanka, India, Cambodia, Singapore, Taiwan, China, Malaysia, Hong Kong, Japan, and Korea.

# Batik Decorations

Batik is a very elegant and classic type of oriental visual art. It is the folk art of waxing and dyeing of cloth. The word *batik* is believed to come from an Indonesian word *ambatik* which means "a cloth with little dots." The exact origins of batik are uncertain. Evidence of early batik has been found all over the Middle East, India, Central Asia, and Africa over 2,000 years ago.

Batik is most popular in the form of paintings. Batik paintings cover a variety of images, ranging from wildlife, fruits, and waterfalls to ancient temples, underwater life, and people. It is also used in tapestries, curtains, and tablecloths. Colorful batik accessories can bring a positive radiance into your spa. The striking beauty of batik is indescribable. Introducing batik paintings, tapestries, and linen into your spa menu can lend an elegant and exotic touch.

# Zen Rock Garden

A Zen rock garden can create a feeling of space, impart a sense of order, and instill a spirit of tranquility in your spa. Like a restorative balm, the miniature rock gardens of "nothingness" are antidotes to stresses of modern living. In the inner appreciation of the simplicity of a miniature garden, one has the ability to reduce all complexities to a matter of sand and rocks. The gardens are a means to discover the sources and strengths of the natural humanity, which, according to Zen teaching, is poised, calm, sincere, and capable of facing all matters in life with calmness and perfect composure. A Zen rock garden reduces the complexities of life and helps to develop an inner calm. It makes the stress levels slip away, promoting better health and well-being. Zen rock gardens can puzzle, fascinate, and surprise spa visitors.

# Exotic Paintings and Photographs

Introduce paintings and photographs with oriental overtones to your spa. For example, if your spa offers Ayurveda treatments, the lotus flower is an apt painting to display. Lotus is a sacred flower used in Ayurveda for flower baths, nutrition, and essences. Give an exotic touch by naming each room after an oriental flower or plant, such as the Lotus Room, the Plumeria Room, and the Coconut Room. Make the room a reflection of the plant itself. For example, the Lotus room can be painted in light purple, which is the color of the flower, and paintings and photographs of Lotus ponds, flowers, and plants can be hung to decorate the space.

Beyond the superficial aesthetics of calling it the Lotus room there lies a deeper significance. The lotus captures the essence of Buddhist thinking. The Lotus root goes deep in the mud and is filled with thorns and dirt. The flower that blooms on the surface however, is stunning. In Buddhist thinking, the lotus is a symbol of life. The foundation of life is pain and suffering, like the root of the lotus. Out of this suffering comes a beautiful state of enlightenment, which is the elegant flower itself. Thus, introducing the image of the lotus not only adds aesthetic pleasure but also lends a deeper, spiritual significance to a client's spa experience.

# Bamboo Flooring and Roofing

Bamboo flooring and roofing have become fashionable in recent years. They can render a beautiful and elegant design element to your spa. Bamboo makes an attractive, stable, and dent-resistant alternative to wood flooring and roofing. Visually, bamboo roofing creates a more soothing sensation than a concrete ceiling does. While receiving a massage for example, clients can experience visual healing therapy by enjoying the aesthetics of bamboo roofing. If your spa already has a concrete ceiling, the round shaped sections of bamboo can be bound together and hung as decoration. Adding colored lighting further enhances the intimacy of bamboo roofing.

Based largely on its high growth rate, bamboo is promoted as a "green" building material. Bamboo, which is actually a grass, is the fastest growing plant on earth and is a renewable resource. Oak takes 120 years to grow to maturity, but bamboo can be harvested in three to seven year cycles. Bamboo is especially useful for eco-friendly or green spas, which use sustainable products for construction.

# Coconut Ornaments

Coconut ornaments are a simple and effective way of giving an oriental touch to your spa. Coconut is a staple food in most Asian countries. Ornaments made from the coconut are fairly inexpensive. Coconut leaves, bark, and shells are used for decorations, utensils, and roofing. A simple decoration is the hard shell coconut itself, with "Do Not Disturb" painted on it and placed outside the rooms.

# Haiku Meditation Center

Haiku is a type of Japanese poetry. A predominant theme of haiku poetry is nature and the relationship between nature and man. Haiku is also a Japanese style of building that enhances the human connection with nature. Reminiscent of 16th-century Japanese country houses, haiku building structures use pole-and-beam architecture and are custom crafted from the finest woods. Haiku-style lodgings are suitable for all climates. Haiku building structures have simple elegance and beauty, making them priceless in their potential for peace, tranquility, and harmony. Introduce a haiku meditation center into your spa, filled with open space, luscious ponds, and free flow of air. It can enhance the quietude and serenity of the meditation space.

# Clay Pot of Water

A traditional Sri Lankan village custom is to have a clay pot resembling a birdbath at the entrance to living spaces. Each morning villagers fill the pot with fresh flower petals and coins. It is a daily vow, asking the spiritual forces for purity, new beginnings, and prosperity. "May all those who enter this space be filled with pure hearts, and may they be renewed with cleanliness when they leave" is uttered subconsciously, as fresh flower petals are added to the clay pot. Changing the water is symbolic of detaching from negative thoughts and replacing them with positive ones. The coins are a way for villagers to ask for prosperity and abundance.

# Facemasks

Facemasks are an integral part of the Asian cultural heritage. Wooden facemasks perform a variety of roles in most Asian healing ceremonies. Firstly, they are believed to chase away evil spirits and replace the living space with gods. Secondly, facemasks perform the role of warding off the evil eye. It is believed that facemasks have the power to change a negative thought into a positive one, thereby casting off the evil eye. Thirdly, facemasks are hung for aesthetic value. They are beautiful, arresting, and sensual.

# Rice Paper Décor

Rice is grown throughout Asia, and rice paper is made from the pith of the rice-paper plant, *Tetrapanax papyriferus*. The manufacture of rice paper originated in China. Today, it has spread to other parts of Asia, where rice paper is used for painting and calligraphy.

Some Chinese candies come wrapped in edible rice paper. Rice paper can also be used in a roofing decorations, curtains, and tapestries. Chinese lanterns, dragons, and zodiac signs made from rice paper can add an elegant oriental touch to your spa.

# Oriental Music

Indian sitar music, Japanese music, Chinese music, and Javanese Gamelan music are some examples that can add exotic sounds to your spa. Recordings of oriental music can be purchased from most record stores in the world music or ethnomusicology section. However, a better way to get authentic sounds is to buy tapes during a visit to Asia. If you are planning to visit, take advantage of the opportunity and buy a good selection of local music while you are there.

# Oriental Drinks

Introduce oriental fruit juices into your spa menu. When a client comes in for a spa treatment, greet him or her with an exotic drink. A wonderful summery drink that

## Tamarind Juice

*Ingredients*
 250 g. (90 oz.) tamarind
 1.2 liter (2 pints) water
 3 tablespoons lemon juice
 400 g. (14oz) sugar

*Preparation*
1. Break up the dry tamarind into small pieces. Place in a large bowl, cover with water and soak for ten hours.
2. Boil the tamarind in a saucepan for 5 minutes. Remove any froth that may form.
3. Pour through sieve and discard the seeds.
4. Return to saucepan and add sugar. Mix on low heat until the mixture begins to thicken.
5. Add lemon juice and boil for 5 minutes.
6. Pour the liquid through a sieve. Leave to cool for one hour. Place in refrigerator for one hour.

is more refreshing than lemonade is tamarind juice. In the past, tamarind was an exotic item found only in Asian and Caribbean food stores. Today, however, it has entered the mainstream. Fresh tamarind pods can be found in the Oriental aisle of some grocery store chains. The medicinal uses of the tamarind are many. Tamarind is used in Sri Lanka and India as part of Ayurveda treatments.

# Starting a
# Day Spa

A day spa is a place that you visit for the day to get massages, facials, and skin and body treatments. Day spas do not offer overnight facilities and typically do not offer food services either. They come in a wide range of styles and personalities—from small village spas to 40,000-square-foot extravaganzas.

The Day Spa Association defines a day spa as follows:

*Day spas are full service facilities offering an array of spa treatments administered by licensed and certified spa technicians. They may be stand-alone facilities, many incorporated in or adjacent to a salon, be part of a bustling city hotel, or connected to a health club. In addition, many spas are becoming allied with a one-stop wellness center or an adjunct to medical facilities such as rehabilitation centers, dermatology clinics, plastic surgeons, chiropractors, or even complementary medical practitioners.*

According to a 2004 industry report published by The Spa Association, day spas continue to be the strongest segment of the spa industry in North America. More and more people are opening day spas—and making large profits, too.

If you are thinking about starting a day spa, it is important to get to know the marketplace. Visit as many spas as possible and get an idea of what types of day spas are out there. This also gives you direct feedback on the cutting-edge technology that prevails in the day spa environment and what kind of services you ought to be offering at your day spa. Take the time to think everything through—from your long-term goals, to cash flow, to creating a wet room, and to the amount of laundry your spa will go through every week. All the big and small details make a difference. Networking with other spa owners and body workers will help your business to thrive. Not only do they help with generating industry resources, but they also place a more human face on the whole money-and-business component of owning a spa.

### Stat Fact

In 1987 there were 30 day spas in the United States, according to the Spa Expert at the Marshall Plan, a Venice, California-based communications firm specializing in spas and resorts. By 1997 the number had exploded to 600 day spas.

Creating an attractive service menu card can help to boost your sales and entice new customers. This can be in the form of a single card or in the form of a spa brochure. Remember to publish your menu of services on the web as well.

# A Day Spa for Men

If you are thinking about opening a day spa, consider introducing treatments for the gents. This is a rapidly booming and underexplored area in the day spa business. Be sure you have a thorough understanding of what men want in a spa. Be well versed on male skin conditions and the best products for treating them. You will also need to know exactly what type of services appeal to them and the best way to introduce them in your spa environment.

# Sunshine Day Spa Service Menu

*The Sunshine Facial*: 35 min./60 min. /80 min.  $65 / $125 / $145

This is especially for men. A man's skin is thicker and subject to more aggravation than a woman's skin. At Sunshine Spa, we use formulas that contain a higher percentage of active ingredients to better treat men's skin. These products have ingredients to give sure-fire results. The Sunshine Facial will treat you like a king, surpassing your expectations and leaving you wanting more.

*Sunshine Touch Up for Men*: 30 min. $60

Perhaps you are not a happy guy when it comes to your hands. Rough and beat up cuticles and hands don't make you feel good about yourself. Sunshine Touch Up will fix that. We will exfoliate and soften this area using certified organic scrubs and fruit enzymes and then apply a hydrating mask to soften and soothe the edges.

*Bodywraps*: 60 min. $50

Our unique refreshing wraps will totally destress your body and at the same time perk you up. It's also a great way to detoxify and shape your body. Let our therapists work on your body and you will know why it is one of our best-selling treatments, especially with the ladies. Some of our wraps include (1) thermal lime wrap, (2) sea weed mud wrap, and (3) anti-cellulite wrap.

*The Therapeutic Hydrotherapy*: 20–50 min. $85

A spa experience would not be complete without stimulating hydrotherapy. Using the latest underwater massage technology and herbal ingredients such as mineral salts, ginseng, and green tea, you will feel rejuvenated after each session. A great way to unwind after a hard day's work.

*Waxings*: $20–$120

Try our delightful waxings for specific parts of the body.

Your décor needs to suit the needs of men. Use masculine colors and introduce lighting, sculpture, landscaping, and music that appeal to men. Keep your spa environment clean, simple, and uncluttered. Your spa brochure needs to have a touch of masculinity as well. Incorporate visuals that reinforce spa treatments for males—posters of men receiving a foot massage, trade journals for men, and photography of male models are examples. If you would like to attract both men and women, then designate a certain area of your spa for men and another for women only. That way you target a part of your services for women and the rest for men.

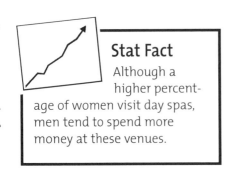

**Stat Fact**

Although a higher percentage of women visit day spas, men tend to spend more money at these venues.

Men are more faithful to a facility than their female counterparts who tend to try every new place that opens. Depending on the marketing emphasis and location of a day spa facility, some claim a 50 percent male clientele. The International Spa Association reported in a recent survey that 28 percent of its members' clients are men. Their number-one choice of service is the massage, followed by pedicures and facials.

# Teen Spas

Teens are a growing market that will help define the future day spa industry. The teen population seeking cosmetic treatments continues to rise, especially at day spas. Day spas throughout the country are seeing an influx of teenage girls who are drawn by the beauty treatments and the glamor of a luxurious day spa experience. Right now, the majority of teens visiting day spas are females. In the years to come, however, there is likely to be an influx of teen boys as well.

Study the fashion trends, make-up, hair styling, and skin care products that are showcased in teen magazines and deliver the services that appeal to teens. If you or any of your staff members have teenage children, get as much feedback from them as possible. The direct feedback that you can get from teenagers can become invaluable in your marketing efforts to this group. Ask as many questions as you can from teenagers themselves: What type of treatments do you like? How do you like those treatments delivered? What are the current hair styling trends?

## Selling Day Spa Services to Teens

Teenagers want multiple distractions in order to stay focused. Offer them what they want. Create a spa environment that allows teens to multitask. For example, create a setting where teenagers can use their iPods, instant message on their Blackberries, and watch You Tube simultaneously while receiving a massage.

What most teens are seeking is someone to talk to. Although there is no harm in listening to what they have to say, therapists must be advised to not get involved in the personal affairs of teens. Train your massage therapist to listen, but not start playing the role of mother, priest, or psychologist during treatments. Create an environment where teens feel comfortable enough to talk in your day spa but not expect counseling or therapist services in return. Teens look for guidance but at the same time want to assert their independence.

Peer pressure is a primary factor with teens. Teens are vulnerable. For example, getting into self-esteem or weight-loss issues can get you into trouble. Train your staff workers to tread with caution when touching on such topics.

Teens tend to have limited disposable incomes. They are more into spending than saving. Keeping this in mind, offer treatments and products that are good value for their money.

Many spas have age restrictions when it comes to certain services, such as massage therapy for teens. Some age restrictions may be mandated by state and local laws. If you decide to offer your treatments to teens, find out the specific laws designated for your state and proceed with caution.

# The Mobile Spa: A Day Spa at Your Doorstep

Consumers are busier then ever. They are increasingly seeking opportunities to pamper themselves in their own surroundings. Bring the spa experience to your clients via a mobile day spa, the popular craze of pampering guests at their doorsteps. Mobile spa treatments can be offered in private homes, offices, or hotels. With the proper crew and right attitude, you will be running a successful mobile spa business in no time.

A mobile spa is comprised of a network of traveling spa professionals and offers the essentials in day spa treatments—facials, massage, bridal hair and make-up, body treatments, manicures, and pedicures—with an atmosphere of tranquility just like in a regular spa. As a mobile spa owner, you have the luxury of offering spa services typically offered at day spas in the comfort of your client's home, office, hotel, or lounge.

Mobile spas are especially appealing to working women, allowing them to relax after a stressful workweek. They are also a flexible way for women to bond with their girlfriends. At a day spa, it is virtually impossible for a group of women to be scheduled at the same time, but a mobile spa allows this flexibility for group packages.

To comply with various state health regulations, not all services are legal in every location. For example, in some states it is illegal to perform manicures/pedicures and certain facials outside of a stationary salon/spa. So, check with your state licensing board to find out the legalities involved in mobile spa operations.

The benefits of mobile spas are:

- In 30 minutes or less, a home, hotel room, office, studio, rooftop, poolside cabana, or whatever space you choose can be transformed into a luxurious day spa.
- Spa packages are a relaxing and private spa day for individuals, couples' retreats,

# Reasons to Go "Spaless" with Mobile Spas

In general, mobile spa costs are competitive with those at traditional day spas. Mobile spas are a great way to work on your own terms, without being overseen by a boss every step of the way. Here are some of the benefits for individuals thinking about starting mobile spas:

1. *Unlimited income.* The harder you work and promote your business, the more money you make, rather than "punching a clock" for 40 hours a week.

2. *Freedom and flexibility.* You will have the freedom to schedule appointments around family and other commitments.

3. *Booming industry.* The mobile spa business is still in its infant stage. Its potential is yet unexplored. This is your chance to capitalize on this opportunity.

4. *Low start-up costs.* No ongoing costs like those involved in operating a storefront operation—rent, utilities, maintenance, higher insurance, and business taxes.

5. *Ability to experiment.* Mobile spas offer limited risk. You can tread the waters before complete immersion. Don't quit your day job just yet. Keep your present job while you build a clientele or start working full time with your business. At the start, you can offer mobile spa treatments in the evenings, after you have worked at your day job.

6. *Tax advantages.* You can claim legitimate business expenses relating to your vehicle, supplies, and "home office."

7. *Career satisfaction.* You are building your very own business based on your own skills and initiative.

8. *Independence.* You are truly on your own and not subject to the demands of an employer.

9. *Creativity.* You can use your imagination to create interesting and effective ideas for your business, such as including aromatherapy candles, incense, flower petals, and soft music during your treatments.

10. *Variety.* You are released from the boredom of a predictable day-to-day job. No two days will ever be the same. You are out in the community, not stuck working in a spa or salon. You will experience different scenery everyday.

11. *Mobile retail shop.* You can become a traveling salesman through a mobile retail shop. Carry a retail shop with skin care products and accessories such as herbal neck wraps, spa slippers, and ointments for your clients, and they are likely to provide you with a side income.

weddings, corporate incentives, full-scale spa events, and more.

- No traffic jams or parking issues for the customer.
- No worries or stress of making it to the appointment on time.
- A great way to have fun and relax with the people you like to spend time with.

Target population groups for mobile spas are:

- Clients who are working from home do not have the time to go to a spa.
- Clients who prefer their personal surroundings and do not feel comfortable getting personalized treatments in an outside environment.
- Clients who are not physically able to get themselves out of the house due to temporary/permanent illnesses.
- Office workers who want a break during a high-stress period.
- Hotel guests who seek a relaxing treatment while in transit.
- Elderly people who cannot leave their homes.
- New mothers who are caring for their infants and unable to leave their homes even for short periods of time.

# Mobile Spa Etiquette

Always deliver a copy of your mobile spa etiquette rules before the treatment begins at a site. This can save you from unwanted situations arising before, during, or after a treatment. Your spa etiquette can be printed on a menu sheet and be hand delivered. If you have a web site, post it online for clients to review. Here are some sample guidelines for your spa etiquette:

- *Reservation policy.* Reservations need to be made at least 24 hours in advance. Reservations can be made by phone or through the online contact form on our web site. There is a $75 minimum for services. A destination fee applies as well.
- *Cancellation policy.* For individual services, we require at least 24 hours notice when canceling an appointment. There is a 20 percent charge for cancellations made less than 24 hours in advance. Changes to any packages must also be made 24 hours prior to the appointment.
- *Gratuities.* If you are pleased with the services you have received, it is customary to give a 15 to 20 percent gratuity to your spa technician.
- *Age requirement.* Clients must be at least 16 years of age.
- *Punctuality.* Our spa professionals will arrive 15 to 20 minutes prior to your appointment to set up. We carry it all—from tables to candles to speaker systems.
- *Health regulations.* We do not treat you if you have open wounds, incisions, and other contagious health conditions; if you are intoxicated; or if you harass our staff.

# Spa Parties: You Are Invited

Imagine giving your clients a massage under a beautiful shady tree, by a pool, next to a Jacuzzi, or even under the twinkling stars on a clear summer night. The sound of soothing music in the background, flickering candlelight, and the scent of soothing lavender to calm the soul are pleasant additions that can make the atmosphere truly magical. Guess what? You have just created the setting for a spa party for your clients and they are loving it.

Spa parties are the hottest craze in the spa industry. They add mini-spa treatments at the location of your guest's choice, indoors or out. Indulge your clients as your team of licensed spa professionals turn a home, office, patio, or hotel into a soothing oasis.

A spa party is a type of mobile spa, and a touch of creativity makes each one unique. The spa party concept is still in the infant stage, showing a lot of promise toward growth. As a future spa owner, you have great potential to capture this largely unexplored niche. A spa party is a form of a mobile spa and can be thrown in the comfort of a client's home. Each party can be customized according to your customer's theme and interest. As the spa owner, it is your responsibility to have a dedicated spa director

---

## Party Time

Spa parties can be thrown for the following events:

- ○ Bachelorette parties
- ○ Corporate events
- ○ Employee appreciation days
- ○ Wellness parties
- ○ Bridal showers
- ○ Office parties
- ○ Birthdays
- ○ Graduations
- ○ Anniversaries
- ○ Promotions
- ○ Pre-prom pampering
- ○ Baby showers
- ○ Fundraising events
- ○ Any reason get-togethers

---

and on-site facilitator who consults, develops, attends, and manages every aspect of your event, along with a complete staff of certified/licensed and insured technicians to provide your services.

Some reasons why clients love spa parties are:

- People do not have the time to go to the spa.
- When clients *do* have time to make it to a stationary spa, it may be already be booked by other clients and they are unable to get an appointment when they want.
- The drive back home from the spa to their home base removes the relaxed feeling that they get after the spa treatment. It is like "money for nothing."
- It is hard to coordinate a group package for several friends or to organize a spa party at business venues.

# Party Ideas

Here are some ideas to make your spa party special:

- Introduce the right decor, ambience, and spa attire
- Create invitation cards
- Order catering services
- Serve cocktails
- Make exciting gift bags
- Have party games
- Hire DJs and music
- Offer skin care and massage seminars
- Organize classes on how to roll sushi
- Have a tarot card and palm reader present
- Organize karioke events
- Offer food and wine tasting
- Offer aromatherapy at no extra charge
- Provide gift certificates
- Offer yoga sessions
- Have hands-on demonstrations on how to make natural spa treatments at home and self-massage techniques
- Light up the space with fragrant candles
- Have your staff wear interesting costumes. For example, on Halloween wear something funky
- Use color therapy such as soft lighting, colorful balloons, and tie-dye tapestries

Some necessities that spa owners should provide for spa parties are:

- Massage table
- Massage lotion/oil
- Portable CD player w/CDs
- Aromatherapy oils
- Aromatic candles
- Sheets for massage table
- Skin care products for facials
- Towel warmer
- Body mud
- Manicurists bring all, including nail polish and foot tubs for pedicures

# Nail and Hair Salons

An afternoon spent being manicured and pedicured is quite relaxing. It should leave your clients feeling pampered and regal. Because our hands and feet correspond to the systems and structures throughout our entire body, attention to these extremities is like attention to the whole body.

Nail salons offer a variety of services, including manicures, pedicures, paraffin treatments, and hand and foot massages. Some nail salons offer hair cutting services as well. Manicures and pedicures by professionals are common treatments, often accompanied by long hand and foot soaks, lotions, oils, and lots of detailed care with brushes, files, emery boards, buffers, polishes, and even mini-massages.

Haircuts are the most popular service in hair salons. Hair styling includes styles created with a blow dryer, rollers, and curling iron, among other equipment. Hair salons also offer coloring services. Hair texturing services include permanent waves, perms, braiding, and anti-curl treatments.

# Tanning Salons

Starting your own tanning salon is a great way to get into the day spa business. With growing awareness being given to skin cancer caused by the sun's UV rays, more and more people are turning to sunless tanning salons as a practical alternative for getting that natural, golden glow. Customers getting bronzed at tanning salons are on the rise. The drive some people have to get a tan is as powerful and all-consuming as the impulse of others to lose weight fast, thicken thinning hair, and restore youth through

# How to Minimize Risks of Tanning

If you decide to start a tanning salon, it is important to minimize your clients' exposure in order to avoid burning. Here are some points to pay attention to:

○ Does the device manufacturer recommend exposure limits for the skin type of each client?

○ Is there a timer you can set on the tanning device that automatically shuts off the lights or somehow signals you regarding your exposure time? Remember, exposure time effects burning. UV dosage, whether received in a few large doses or in many smaller ones over a long period of time, can cause skin cancer and premature aging.

○ When using a tanning device, it is important to use eye protection because UV light can harm the corneas without your being aware of any injury. When you offer eye protection, make it mandatory for clients to wear them. They need to fit snugly. Your salon needs to sterilize the goggles after each use to prevent the spread of eye infection. Studies show that too much exposure to ultraviolet rays, including UVA rays, can damage the retina. Over-exposure can burn the cornea, and repeated exposure over many years can change the structure of an eye lens. It begins to form a cloud, forming a cataract. The Food and Drug Administration requires tanning salons to direct all customers to wear protective eye goggles.

anti-aging treatments. Sunless tanning is no longer a fashion, rather, it has become an attitude, even a lifestyle.

The most popular device used in tanning salons is a clamshell-like tanning bed. The customer lies down on a Plexiglass surface and relaxes as lights from above and below reach the body.

Always consult your clients' medical histories and maintain any pertinent information on file. Have the staff update it periodically. Here are some questions to ask when considering clients' medical histories:

• Are you undergoing treatment for lupus or diabetes, or are you susceptible to cold sores? These conditions can be severely aggravated if you are exposed to ultraviolet radiation from tanning devices, sunlamps, or natural sunlight.

• Do you use antihistamines, tranquilizers, birth control pills, and other medications that are known to increase the likelihood of rashes, sunburns, and other allergic-type reactions when used with the sun or artificial light?

# Benefits of Sunless Tanning

To market your tanning services, highlight why the public should get tans. Here are some points to bring up:

- As concerns over the harmful effects of the sun's UV rays grow, sunless tanning has emerged as the safest and most effective way of giving your skin that summery look.

- Sunless tanning is an effective anti-aging treatment. Some of the wrinkling, sagging, rough skin texture or irregular skin colorations are *not* caused by aging but through exposure to the sun's ultraviolet rays.

- It is an indisputable fact that the sun can cause skin cancer. The sun's UV rays permanently damage your skin. This is another reason why tanning salons are popular.

- Tanning salons have different kinds of treatments to give beautiful, natural color that bronzes the body beautifully.

- Sunless tans take less time than a real tan; you can have a tan tomorrow.

- You don't have to start "working on your tan" months in advance. A sunless tan can be a spontaneous decision, like trying a new nail polish.

- Sunless tanners are better now than they have ever been. Sunless tans are safe.

- Sunless tans are temporary. If your customers are unhappy with the look, the tan will be completely gone within a few days. A sunless tan is not a long term commitment. It fits well with a disposable lifestyle.

- Sunless tanning is a practical alternative to sunbathing.

# Starting a
# Destination Spa

A destination spa is a place where clients come for relaxation, healing, and beauty treatments. They offer all-inclusive treatments ranging from yoga to weight-loss programs. Clients may spend one day to a week (or even longer) at these spas. Rates can vary from $500 to $25,000 a week, or more. A food service is included in destination spas where spa cuisine becomes a central focus of the healing and wellness programs. Examples of destination spas include resort spas, hotel spas, and cruise ship spas.

# Steps to Consider When Starting a Destination Spa

Whether opening, expanding, or remodeling a spa, it is crucial that business owners consider the impact a carefully designed spa has on profitability. Certain steps should be taken by entrepreneurs to guarantee a successful spa design that will garner long-term results. The main steps of starting a destination spa are:

- Licensing regulations
- Health and safety regulations
- Space planning
- Spa layout
- Establishing an identity
- Retail space
- Quality hardware
- Décor
- Outdoor landscaping

## Licensing Regulations

Whether you are a licensed spa professional, such as a licensed aesthetician, cosmetologist, or plastic surgeon, or a prospective business developer or real estate mogul looking to open a new destination spa, the first place you should go for answers about operating a destination spa business is your state licensing board. Laws pertaining to destination spas vary from state to state. Before you purchase equipment or hire staff, be sure you understand exactly which individual licenses and permits are necessary for opening a spa in your state, the limits of those licenses, and your responsibility when it comes to having other professionals, such as medical personnel, perform services on your premises.

## Health and Safety Regulations

As a destination spa owner, you need to pay special attention to matters related to health and consumer protection. Your spa services must comply with the standards of the Occupational Safety and Health Administration (OSHA). This federal agency oversees safety in the workplace. OSHA supplies those in the health care and personal care industries with specific guidelines to prevent the transmission of diseases. Your state licensing board and the local board of health will also have criteria for public health and hygiene with which you must comply. Violations are often made public and could ruin your spa business.

# Space Planning

Before any building takes place or before choosing a location, space planning should be outlined in detail. This entails the use of specific areas of the overall space and maximizes the highest per-square-foot revenue on the investment. It also offers a map of the client experience and the traffic flow. Space planning must ensure client satisfaction and comfort.

# Spa Layout

Designing your spa is likely to be one of the more exciting tasks that you encounter in developing your spa business. The layout of your spa can make or break your business venture. A quality design calls for expert knowledge in the areas of architecture, construction, interior design, marketing, products, and equipment. If you have the quality and expertise in these areas, then follow your judgment. Most people, however, will have to seek outside help. Before you engage an architect, designer, or contractor, you need to be clear about your goals and objectives, the costs involved, and your budget. Whatever your focus is, the design of your destination spa should ultimately be one that generates financial success and profitability.

When starting a destination spa, one of the key components you need to pay attention to is layout. Spending money properly in the design and layout stages will quite literally save you thousands (and maybe even millions) when the construction crews and contractors move in to install the electrical, plumbing, and mechanical components of the spa. Never underestimate the value of a thorough set of plans. They are the blueprints from which you will be fleshing out the large and small details. Because these plans will form the basis of contractors' bids, incomplete drawings could distort those bids to your disadvantage. Draw everything up and get written estimates for every aspect of the spa during every stage of its progress. Prior to any element of construction, every light switch, drain, and tile should be accounted for.

A good architect can help to make your dream a reality. A bad architect, on the other hand, can turn it into a nightmare. Although it is not necessary that an architect have experience in planning a spa, it makes sense to choose one with experience in medical and recreational environments with some of the design features found in spas. Another option is to hire an architectural firm or a spa consulting service. It is best to retain an architectural firm that specializes in spa design. If the architect is unfamiliar with the operations of a spa business, many important areas could be overlooked. If your architect has little or no spa design experience, make sure the spa consultant and architect work together on design details in order to meet operational and aesthetic needs.

# Establishing Identity

The choice of which type of spa to open should be based on the need identified by market research. These findings will determine what type of spa would best suit the desires of the potential clientele and reap the most profits.

Once a facility type has been selected, it is time to establish its identity and determine the type of client experience the spa team members will create. The types of services offered and the kind of clientele that you hope to attract will define a major part of establishing identity. The client's experience is the foundation of any spa. When planning a spa, the client's experience and the daily spa operation must flow smoothly. There needs to be a balance between the two.

# Retail Space

When designing a destination spa, leave room for retail space. Merchandising is an important function of a destination spa. Your retail space should be a place where clients can browse, relax, and not feel pressured by a receptionist or gift clerk.

Offer products that complement the treatments in your spa. Make your retail space intimate, spacious, and aesthetically appealing. Shelving and counter space should be arranged in a warm and inviting way so that clients are free to walk through aisles without bumping into things. When possible, offer testing products such as perfumes and massage oils that clients can try before purchasing.

Make your reception and retail areas welcoming, soothing, and relaxing. Set up your retail shelves to entice the senses. Use color lighting, music, and sculpture to make your retail space a work of art. Creatively display bath and body products such as salts, candles, soaps, and skin care products. Use attractive glassware to display your retail products. Clean the glassware and furniture on a regular basis to give a shiny feel to the retail space.

Creatively display retail skin care products. For example, if one product contains rose, display some fresh roses next to it. If you are offering a massage vibrating chair for sale, give a free trial run for guests to experience the comfort of sitting in one. It will provide a unique display element that will entice guests to buy or consider that option later on. Offer layaway plans to guests when possible.

# Quality Hardware

Depending on the level of the destination spa you want to start, select the type of hardware that best suits your needs. Avoid installing cheap, mediocre hardware, as it will tarnish over time. It is smarter to invest a little bit more on quality hardware, which will give you years of trouble-free service. Inexpensive faucets, toilet fittings, and door handles that will degrade prematurely under the client traffic volumes you experience will denigrate the look you have created.

# Décor and Landscaping

Both indoors and outdoors, select décor and landscaping that fit the mood of your spa. Incorporating the right décor and landscaping at the start can help you save valuable dollars down the road. Support your décor with tasteful sculpture, lighting, visual art, and color. In addition, hiring a professional decorator can develop a cohesive theme throughout the space. Keep in mind that a spa experience should stimulate all of the senses—sight, sound, touch, taste, and smell.

# Starting a
# Medical Spa

The union between medicine and spas is relatively new in our modern experience. However, "medical spas," or "medi spas," as they are called, have been common throughout history. In centuries past, patients received massages, backrubs, and flower baths as a part of the routine of staying in hospitals. In the ancient capital city of Anuradhapura, Sri Lanka, for example, the ruins of an ancient hospital consist of medicinal boats, walking meditation centers, and flower beds dating back to the times when Buddhism was first introduced to the island in the 3rd century B.C. are an example of a medical spa.

Today, there has been a revival of interest in this ancient practice. People are revisiting that wisdom and have coined a sophisticated name, medical spa. Medical spas are a progressive way of going retro. They acknowledge the wisdom of ancestors that one secret to good health is pampering the body, mind, and soul, through the three "M"s of good health: massage, medicine, and meditation.

The International Medical Spa Association defines a medical spa as:

> *A medical spa is a facility that operates under the full-time, on-site supervision of a licensed health care professional. The facility operates within the scope of practice of its staff, and offers traditional, complementary, and alternative health practices and treatments in a spa-like setting. Practitioners working within a medical spa will be governed by their appropriate licensing board, if licensure is required.*

Still in an infant stage of development, contemporary medical spas are somewhat controversial among medical and non-medical professionals. There are many variations on the definition of medical spa, and the industry is striving to come up with a widely acceptable definition.

According to a November 2006 study conducted by The International Spa Association, there were 310 registered medical spas in 2004, which rose to 915 medical spas by 2006. Entrepreneur.com named the medical spa as one of the top five business opportunities of 2003.

The medical spa is where traditional hospital medicine and alternative therapies cross paths to offer healing and wellness. Medical spa services integrate both traditional and nontraditional medicine with spa treatments. They represent the crossroads where intense medical focus and the power of alternative and complementary therapies combine to create a comprehensive and integrative approach to healing. Medical spas offer treatments for many ailments, including arthritis, skin diseases, weight loss, asthma, migraines, and depression. The medical spa industry embraces the social, psychological, spiritual, physical, and behavioral components of health care and aims toward the achievement of wholeness. It is a logical and convenient evolution in health care that brings together services that promote total well-being.

One of the fundamental differences between a medical spa and a modern day hospital is that in the former clients are not made

## Stat Fact

The American Academy of Cosmetic Surgery (AACS) announced the results of its 2006 Consumer Perception Survey, which showed that 6 percent of adults have had plastic surgery, and nearly 20 percent aspire to do so at some point in their lives.

to feel like patients. Rather, they are made to feel like guests needing their batteries recharged and not fixed. This difference in attitude affects a person's well-being in an important way. The patient is restored on a long-term basis and not just fixed just for that moment. The medical spa also teaches patients how to take care of themselves after they leave the premises.

The medical spa reinforces the importance of a relaxing atmosphere. Attention to detail is essential, from the color of the walls to the fabric of the robes. A soothing, comforting ambience helps to put the client at ease for even the most uncomfortable medical procedures.

Unlike a regular spa, where the main goal is to be pampered, going to a medical spa is not just about pampering and feeling good. Medical spas are becoming more than just places to receive aesthetic services. They combine the modern medical technologies, coupled with lifestyle classes, nutrition programs, wellness services, and effective skin and body care as part of a holistic approach to living a healthy life. Clients can experience one-stop shopping under the same roof for facials, manicures, massages, nutritional advice, and cosmetic procedures.

Professionals who are venturing into this billion-dollar industry include plastic surgeons, ob/gyns, dermatologists, opthalmologists, and even family practitioners. By linking itself to the hospital, it has beneficial effects for both the hospital and spa industries. Many medical spas strive to offer medical care in a comforting, nonclinical environment and complementary therapies in the reassuring context of Western medicine. In essence, the medical spa is a cross between a day spa and a medical office.

Medical spas are now being developed from both the medical and spa ends of the business. Some dermatologists and plastic surgeons expand their practices by hiring estheticians and massage therapists and adding spa-like services, while some day spas are expanding into medical spas by recruiting physicians, ob/gyns, and other medical professionals.

At present, the clinical services available in medical spas are mostly focused on anti-aging and appearance, from botox injections to cellulite firming. In addition to medical procedures that target these areas, the services include stress reduction, skin care, and other preventive health measures. People love one-stop health and beauty shopping. The fusion of the credibility of a medical office with the comfort, services, and personal attention of a day spa is very appealing.

# Steps for Opening a Medical Spa

Plenty of opportunities exist for entrepreneurs to take advantage of the medical spa business. But before you jump into this market keep in mind that sound planning is key. If you are looking to enter the medical spa field or expand your current facility

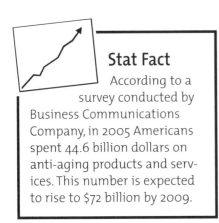

**Stat Fact**

According to a survey conducted by Business Communications Company, in 2005 Americans spent 44.6 billion dollars on anti-aging products and services. This number is expected to rise to $72 billion by 2009.

here are a few steps to consider when planning your business.

# Licensing Regulations

The first and most important step in opening a medical spa is to check with the medical board in your state to determine its position on medical spa treatments. Regulations for medical spas vary from state to state. A doctor generally has to oversee the procedures performed in a medical spa, but this does not mean he or she needs to be physically present on the premises at all times. Find out the rules and regulations that are specific to your state and/or county. Some states have enacted rulings that require medical facilities using a certain level of anesthesia to accredit their facilities. For example, laser resurfacing requires nerve blocks, and a spa offering this service is required to be accredited. The same is true for other medical procedures now being performed in offices and spas outside of hospitals and medical centers. So, it is critical that you have all the licenses in place, whether for business, physician, or staff before planning your spa layout, staffing, and equipment purchasing.

# Signing Contracts

Always have an attorney review documents before signing any contracts. Opening a medical spa can be a sensitive issue in certain areas of the industry, especially because there is a great deal of controversy in the field. Having an attorney on your side right from the start is always a good idea. This can prevent you from getting into legal trouble down the road.

# Finding Your Niche

Determine which type of medical spa you want to start. Some important categories in the market today include:

- *Plastic surgery medical spas.* These are owned and operated by a physician, or group of physicians, certified by the American Board of Plastic Surgery. In a plastic surgery medical spa, virtually all of a client's esthetic needs can be addressed.
- *Dermatology medical spas.* These provide skin care treatments and medical spa services under the supervision of a board-certified dermatologist.
- *Laser centers.* Esthetic lasers are usually the most lucrative treatments available for any medical spa.

- *Dental spa.* In its logical and simplest form, a dental spa is a dental practice that offers spa services. During one appointment, clients can get their teeth whitened plus have microdermabrasion for the skin. Many dental spas offer patient-friendly options, such as a selection of soothing music, aromatherapy, portable DVD players, and roofed-in televisions to make the experience less stressful.

## Medical Spa Menu

When considering treatments for your medical spa menu, choose state-of-the-art services with reliable, proven technology that carry a high public demand. Make sure the treatments that you offer are safe, effective, and popular. Offering the right menu of services can generate significant revenue for your medical spa.

Become an investigator. Attend skin care seminars, medical spa conferences, esthetic medical meetings, and tradeshows. Read professional journals, and ask plenty of questions from others in the medical spa industry. Ask manufacturers for evidence that supports any claims they make regarding their equipment. Find out which treatments are offered in medical spas in your area. Get as much information as you can during this investigative stage. Assess your competitors to get a grip on the cutting edge of the business.

With the doctor holding the reins, the developmental stage of creating the menu must include their involvement. The doctor's support of all spa services and products is crucial to the success of a medical spa. The difficulty lies in creating a menu of services that is synergistic with the doctor's way of thinking, yet still a marketable product. Doctors often feel divided with regard to the benefits of certain spa services.

Along with menu service selection, finding the correct ranges of products is a vital part in the development of the medical spa concept. Pharmaceutical companies have just begun designing products solely for medical spas. Dermatological pharmaceutical representatives will allow these new products to be offered in your spa as long as there is a doctor on staff.

## Buying Technology for a Medical Spa

In any field, investments in technology can make or break a business. The medical spa business is no different. Technology is very expensive and is constantly changing. Getting the most cutting edge technology is vital to running a successful medical spa business. As a spa owner, you must evaluate how much revenue any technological purchase can bring in. Aside from the initial financial investment, you must consider the expense of any additional products or equipment required to perform the desired treatment effectively.

Another point to consider when buying technology for a medical spa is the length of its usefulness. What is trendy today might be old news tomorrow. The longevity of a technology must be assessed before making a decision to buy a specific product. Ask yourself how long this procedure will be popular, what type of a clientele you are likely to have for it, and what new scientific developments could render it obsolete. Think ahead before making a major investment in technology.

When evaluating technology, you must engage in preliminary research. Wait on investing in technology until you have done significant research and believe that it is the right fit for your practice, expertise, and location. When selecting a laser for hair removal—or any piece of technological equipment for your spa, for that matter—think about the revenue it can generate per minute, not per treatment. This type of precise thinking and preliminary research can determine whether you are making a sound investment.

Choose technology not only because you think it will be lucrative but also because you have a genuine passion for the results it provides. Money alone should not be the driving force to buying technology. The technology that you choose needs to support what you enjoy doing as well.

# Know Your Clientele

Anticipate customer needs and wants and provide those services to meet their satisfaction. Customers are the ultimate driving force of your medical spa. If you have an existing business, survey your clients to see what services pique their interests. If you want to become a savvy spa owner, you need to have a keen ability to foresee what customers want even before they are aware of it.

Understanding demographics is important. If you plan to offer expensive cosmetic treatments, make sure your surrounding towns and suburbs can afford it. If you are an alternative healing center with a spiritual flair, you probably don't want a location in a downtown financial district.

# Talk to Clients

Often medical professionals fail to give their patients a basic idea of what they should do and what things to expect before, during, and after treatments. Educate your clients as much as you can about what side effects they may experience, what they should do if they feel different, and what precautions to take before, during, and after treatments. This can be extremely beneficial to your clients and also make them feel valued by your spa.

Talk to your clients and give them an idea of the different options available to make their surgeries as painless as possible. Prior to surgery, patients benefit from the addition of yoga stress control and self-image counseling. During surgery, energy work with a Reiki master may be incorporated, or an experienced acupuncturist might take the place of an anesthesiologist. Post treatment may include long-term weight management programs with nutritionists and sessions with personal trainers.

## Medical Spa Staffing

The staffing of the medical spa is an essential element of a successful operation. The licensed therapists or para-medical estheticians require a working knowledge of all medical procedures performed by the doctors. Estheticians are encouraged to spend an afternoon each month with the doctor on staff to gain understanding of the procedures that the doctor performs. Under the doctor's guidance and supervision, the esthetic staff should be thoroughly trained in patient preparation and contraindications for pre- and post-surgical treatments.

So, who is the ideal candidate to work at a medical spa? Ideally, medical spa owners dream of a worker who is licensed to do it all, from makeup, to hydrotherapy, to Botox. But this is hardly ever the case. However, hiring multiqualified employees typically weighs in your favor as a spa owner. When hiring staff, it is advantageous to employ estheticians with varied medical backgrounds. Estheticians who have worked as dermatologist assistants or registered nurses and estheticians with para-medical continuing education courses are definite assets. Experience in a medical setting combined with a healing touch is of great value.

In some medical spas, staff members have to multitask in order to keep the institution running smoothly during hectic times. Having multitrained staff is a valuable resource. For example, an esthetician needs to be trained to give a foot massage, and a therapist must be comfortable reading medical charts and medical orders. For therapists, training and experience in reflexology, structural integration, manual lymph drainage, endermologie, shiatsu, and craniosacral and pregnancy massage are all plusses. As medical spas strive to give their clients all the services they want, they seek employees who can provide as many services as possible. As a savvy spa owner, you should be interested in hiring the worker who is qualified to do more than one thing.

# Popular Medical Spa Treatments

Medical spas offer treatments for face and skin rejuvenation, laser treatment for the elimination of varicose and spider veins, hair removal, Botox®, collagen enhancement, and customized cosmetic and anti-aging skin care services, among others. Some medical spas offer vitamin energy injections, natural weight loss programs, permanent make up, facial specialties, and acne treatments. Here are some of the current medical spa treatments.

# Botox

Botox is now the most commonly performed cosmetic procedure in the United States. It is one of the most popular anti-aging wrinkle treatments in spas throughout the country. Botox stops wrinkles by paralyzing the muscles that constantly crease the skin. The most popular treatment areas are between the eyebrows and wrinkles by the eyes.

A few drops of Botox cosmetic treatments are injected with a tiny needle into the muscle that creates a wrinkle. Botox blocks the nerve impulse from reaching that area, and as a result, the muscle weakens. As the muscle weakens, the skin overlying the muscle relaxes, and the wrinkles in the skin gradually soften and often disappear.

# Cellulite Firming

If you are thinking of opening a medical spa, introducing cellulite treatment programs is an excellent method of increasing your business and clientele. Cellulite firming treatments have become one of the fastest growing services in the medical spa industry.

Cellulite is the lumpy substance resembling cottage cheese that is commonly found on the thighs, stomach, and buttocks. This appearance is much more common in women than men. Although some men may get it, most medical practitioners have found that 90 to 98 percent of cellulite cases occur among women. Water retention, circulation problems, and dietary factors that include food additives, chemical preservatives, and hormones are usually given as the common causes of cellulite.

Medical spas offer services to lessen the appearance of cellulite with a number of medical treatments. Several machines on the market such as endermologie and synergie stretch the skin and dermal ligaments with rollers and vacuum force. As the ligaments are stretched, they lengthen, thereby relaxing the dimples. The overall effect is to give a smoother appearance to the skin.

Subcision with special needles can also help minimize cellulite by cutting the dermal ligaments tying the skin down. After the skin is released, it rebounds and the cellulite dimpling is improved. The patient's own fat is then injected to prevent the dermal ligaments from re-attaching to the skin. This treatment is time consuming and expensive.

# Laser Hair Removal

Before finalizing on any technology for laser hair removal, first determine the kind of market that you may have for this service. Providing a faster solution than electrology and a more permanent alternative to waxing, laser hair removal has become much safer, more comfortable, and more effective in recent years. Some physicians and medical spas report that laser hair removal has been their best investment, while others claim it has been their worst.

# Oxygen Infusion

Oxygen infusion is yet another innovative modality in the anti-aging arena. The technique applies purified, pressurized oxygen to the skin via probe-like hand pieces. The idea originated from pressurized methods of delivering medications and inoculations. Oxygen infusion technology for esthetics utilizes much lower pressure to assist the skin in absorbing vital products, allowing for more profound and expedient results.

# Starting a
# Spiritual Spa

The ultimate goal of a spiritual spa is to enlighten individuals to find inner peace, calmness, and happiness within themselves. Spiritual spas examine a person's inner journey to the mind, body, and soul. Examples of spiritual spas include eco-holistic spas, meditation centers, Reiki healing centers, spa retreats, and yoga centers.

Certain spiritual spa services can be delivered at a stationary spa or in a mobile setting. For example if you are a yoga master, you can either open a studio in the town or city that you live in and have your clients come to you or you can become an itinerant master and go to your clients. If you are unable to afford to buy or lease space, running a mobile spa from the comforts of your home is a viable option.

# Eco-Holistic Spas

Also known as socially responsible spas, green spas, and eco spas, eco-holistic spas are a return to the wisdom of those ancestors who embraced the idea of balance between man and nature. "Spas gone Green" refers to eco-holistic spas that make a concerted effort to impart green, or environmentally sound, strategies to help conserve the earth's rapidly dwindling natural resources and improve the health of the planet. Eco-friendly spas discourage wasteful habits and inspire sustainability. For example, the waters of the world are in great jeopardy. Eco-holistic spas make a conscious effort to take healing with the waters. "Use less towels to consume less water," is an example of a slogan adopted in eco-holistic spas. Some eco-holistic spas make a concerted effort to use indigenous, locally grown and cultivated products for spa and restaurant usage. For example, only locally harvested avocado, citrus, and lavender might be used by the spa. Using local products is considered a green practice because it uses less packaging and ozone-depleting chemicals in their transportation.

Here are some features that distinguish eco-holistic spas from day, destination, and medical spas:

- Are built with environmentally friendly building materials.
- Use complex, water-recycling and purification systems.
- Conserve energy with solar lighting.
- Are roofed with rapidly renewable sources like bamboo.
- Implement water-reclamation areas.
- Cook in organic kitchens and support local agriculture.
- Install nonchemically treated carpeting and furniture.

# Meditation Centers

The purpose of a meditation center is to foster spiritual growth. It is a place that people go to consciously direct their attention and alter their states of consciousness. Traditionally, they have helped people to become more conscious, unfolding their inner light, love, and wisdom. More recently, meditation centers have become valuable venues for finding peaceful oases of relaxation and stress relief in a demanding, fast-paced world. Meditation centers promote psychological changes and quality-of-life enhancement.

People visit meditation centers for various reasons including:

- Healing
- Making new beginnings
- Emotional cleansing and balancing
- Deepening concentration and insight
- Manifesting change
- Developing intuition
- Unlocking creativity
- Exploring higher realities
- Finding inner guidance
- Recovery from alcoholism, drug addiction, sex addiction, shopping addiction, and gambling addiction

Some meditation centers have begun to add a spa component to create a more integrated approach to healing and wellness. They encourage wellness for conditions such as:

- Arthritis
- Asthma
- Chronic pain
- Diabetes
- Gastrointestinal disorders
- Hot flashes
- Hypertension
- Infertility
- Skin disorders
- Respiratory crisis
- Depression
- Panic attacks
- Migraine headaches

# Reiki Healing Centers

Reiki is the healing energy present in nature. In Japanese, *Reiki* means universal life force. More and more people are turning to Reiki to seek calmness, good health, and harmony in their lives. Including Reiki sessions in your menu of services may help increase the number of your spa clients.

Reiki followers believe that health and disease are a matter of the life force being disrupted. Healers do not try to unblock a person's energy but try to channel the energy of the universe so that the person heals. Reiki can be used to clear away or lighten emotional baggage accumulated during life's journey. It also helps to cure physical ailments such as insomnia, migraines, and headaches.

Reiki is a very ancient science rediscovered by Dr. Mikao Usui in the mid-1800s. Dr. Usui added five spiritual principles to Reiki. They are:

1. Just for today do not worry.
2. Just for today do not get angry.
3. Just for today have the attitude of gratitude.
4. Just for today be honest to yourself.
5. Just for today show love and respect for every living thing.

Some practitioners believe that Reiki is a healing technique, while others see it as a spiritual discipline. A third group of people believes that Reiki is a philosophy with its root in the karma theory and compassion. In essence, Reiki is not a technique or a method or a process; it just is.

# Spa Retreats

A retreat is a withdrawal from ordinary activities for time to commune with God, a spiritual force, or a higher power in prayer and reflection. The retreat is an aspect of spirituality that emphasizes time away from one's usual routine and environment. Every human needs time away from daily routine in which to commune with oneself and one's creator, and a retreat gives this opportunity.

The traditional concept of a retreat has typically centered on specific faiths: Benedictine monasteries, Carmelite convents, Ashrams, and Buddhist meditation caves, or *kutis*, are examples. Today, some retreats have been re-shaped with the attachment of spa services. This has made spa retreats not only places of inner exploration but also places of relaxation, massage treatments, and physical wellness. The ethos of the spa retreat is to leave one's habitual surroundings and usual activities for long enough to loosen one's dependence on them.

# Yoga Centers

Yoga is a way of living, a means of achieving health in body, mind, and spirit. Despite its Indian roots, yoga is basically a nondenominational, holistic practice. *Yoga* is a Sanskrit term, roughly meaning "yoke," or "union." Its definition implies uniting the mind, body, and spirit to enhance health and improve the overall quality of life. Yoga has long been known to calm and quiet the mind. In a way, yoga is a style of meditation, the purpose of which is to develop a transcendent sense of peace and clarity of thought.

Yoga centers are becoming more and more popular. Some instructors are itinerant teachers, traveling from one location to another and offering yoga classes.

Occasionally there are grants that are offered to individuals to become certified and for certified teachers to donate yoga classes to groups, thereby spreading yoga into the lives of more and more people. Usually these grants are offered by non-profit organizations, private individuals, and private foundations, not the federal government.

If you are a certified instructor, here are some ways to make a living through the teaching of yoga:

- Open a yoga studio.
- Organize a mobile yoga spa.
- Connect with your local gym to start a weekly yoga class.
- Offer a yoga class at the community campus.
- Organize yoga tours to India.

# Spa Etiquette: Laying Down the Rules

Spa etiquette is the decorum expected at spas, both by employers and consumers. It lets spa guests and employees know how to behave when they are in a spa setting. Some spa owners have their spa etiquette rules posted on their web sites while others have them printed on a bulletin board within the spa premises. Posting your rules for clients to view may save you from unnecessary headaches that can arise from unforeseen situations.

There are some common rules of spa etiquette:

- *Attire*. Wear casual attire that easily slips off and on without fussing. The spa provides robes and slippers for your treatment.
- *Cancellations*. Clients must give 24-hours notice for a spa cancellation refund. Typically, cancellation of packages requires a seven-day notice.
- *Children*. Children under 18 must have written consent from a parent or guardian to receive spa treatments. Some spas don't allow children, while others encourage the presence of children.
- *Communicating with your therapist/healer*. If you are uncomfortable with anything during your treatment, such as the pressure, music, room temperature, or lighting, speak up. Let your therapist know. You can talk during the treatment or stay quiet, as you choose.
- *Gift certificates*. The minimum is usually $50. Gift certificates can be purchased directly from the spa. Typically, gift certificates are nonrefundable but transferable to another person.
- *Jewelry*. Remove neck and wrist ornaments prior to treatment. The spa cannot be responsible for any loss of valuables.
- *Product purchases and returns*. Some spas give full refunds on unopened products; others have a 30-day return policy on retail products.
- *Punctuality*. Clients must arrive 30 minutes prior to their appointments so that they have time to check in, change their clothes or disrobe, and relax. Typically, each guest completes a health history form.
- *Referrals*. Most spas offer specials, promotions, and other incentives to extend their gratitude for clients who make referrals.
- *Shaving*. Beardless men receiving a facial are encouraged to shave at least two hours prior to the treatment. Clients taking a shave are encouraged to shave at least two hours before their appointment. This is especially true in the case of beardless men receiving a facial. It is recommended that clients who have booked a body scrub to shave the day before. Rubbing salt into the slightest razor wound is not a very relaxing experience. For women, it is best to not shave before exfoliation.
- *Sound of silence*. People come to spas to seek quietude and de-stress. Refrain from loud conversation, laughter, and obnoxious behavior. Cell phones are prohibited in most spas. The sound of silence is greatly appreciated.
- *Tipping*. The rule of thumb is 15 to 20 percent of the cost of service. Clients may leave more or less, depending on the quality of the service. Spas usually provide an envelope at the front desk when checking out for clients to place the

gratuity and the therapist's name. In cases where the tip has already been included in your bill, there is no need to double tip. Spa owners must remember that tips are considered part of an employee's taxable income. They are obligated to report them to the IRS.

# Current, Future, and Futuristic Spa Trends

The word spa is becoming a hot marketing buzzword. Spa-inspired tastes and trends have become interwoven into daily life. Unlike most other industries, the image of spas changes almost on a daily basis. What is hot today may be old news tomorrow. Staying up-to-date on spa trends will place you at an advantage as you run your successful business.

# Current Spa Trends

Current spa trends are centered around anti-aging, medical spas, male spas, and the corporate world. The internet plays a pivotal role in connecting consumers with clients in the current spa scene.

## Anti-Aging Products and Services

Anti-aging products and services have become a sign of our times. They symbolize the changing role of skin care. The term *anti-aging* applies to procedures, regimens, products, and technologies designed to reverse and prevent the signs of aging in order to maintain a youthful appearance. This definition encompasses prevention, maintenance, and reversal, and it broadens the range of the clientele from young adults who are beginning to see the initial hints of aging to people who are well into their golden years. Treatments are especially popular with baby boomers who constitute the largest single population group in the country, at 78 million. Many are very interested in anti-aging treatments. The anti-aging skin care field began as a niche market. However, today it has rapidly become an American way of life. These products and procedures are an industry in and of themselves, providing practitioners with virtually limitless earning capability and a perpetually growing client base.

Consumers are seeking anti-aging treatments at a younger age than ever before. Once reserved primarily for mature women, male and female clients now are getting facials regularly—even as teenagers. These clients believe that it is never too early, or too late, to incorporate professional anti-aging treatments and take-home regimens into their lifestyles.

## Spas for Men

The male market will continue to flourish as men buy into the philosophy of looking and feeling good. This trend will manifest itself in an increasing number of spas devoted strictly to providing men with services in a way that protects their privacy and masculinity. Spas will continue to attract men with male-focused offerings, including golf, outdoor-adventure activities, male cosmetic treatments, and high-octane fitness programs.

## Dental Spas

In April 2006, The International Dental Spa Association released a first-of-its-kind study revealing an initial count of the number of dental spas across the United States. The study revealed that 125 to 200 dental spas exist across the nation, and the numbers are growing.

With studies indicating that as many as 12 million Americans balk at visiting a dentist because of fear or anxiety, there is a potentially large pool to tap. Treatments offered at dental spas include acne, tooth whitening, cosmetic dentistry, spa treatments, aromatherapy, massages, and facials.

## Back to the Future

Spas have returned to the wisdom of the ancients and offer older techniques as part of their treatment plans. Ancient Chinese medicine, music therapy, and Ayurvedic-based treatments are age-old tested treatments that have made a comeback in modern day spas.

## The Corporate Connection

Day spas are reaping significant revenue by attracting corporate clients. Corporate meeting planners are using spa grounds as the new conference site. This is an indication that spas have stepped beyond beauty and health treatments. The tertiary component is to combine the socializing and business aspects.

Spas are also becoming more and more a part of day-to-day business life. More people are beginning to mix business with spa pleasure. Private companies, nonprofit organizations, and small business owners are increasingly using spas to build relationships, motivate employees, and manage employee health. Spas serve as a catalyst to improve the quality of life at work.

## Better, Cheaper, Faster

"Better, cheaper, faster" is a slang phrase used in the high-tech industry to explain the speed at which competition drives product improvement. Spas must provide the highest-quality services for their price, in the most efficient time frame, in order to be competitive.

## From Exclusive to Inclusive

Spas are no longer confined to the rich and the aristocracy. Times have changed. From the construction worker who spends the day pouring cement to the billionaire's wife seeking a manicure, all can seek spa treatments at the same site. Spas cater to the average person as well as those with great wealth, thus expanding its marketing potential. The spa experience has become more affordable and inclusive.

# Future Spa Trends

Future spa trends will focus on geriatrics, pediatrics, transitions abroad, accommodating pets, and on offering treatments on commercial airlines.

# Kid Spas

Spas will tailor programs for the entire family, thus including children and infants. Spas will keep pace by offering more family-oriented activities, spas-for-kids, and/or kids-only spa programs. While parents are receiving massages, kids can have a separate play area. As baby boomers become spa lovers and introduce their children to the spa lifestyle, their children, too, become users of spa treatments and products. Baby sitting services, infant massage services, and pediatric care will become a part of the spa experience, thus making spa-going a family event.

# Spas for the Dying

There will be an increase of geriatric treatments catering to the aging population. People are living longer. The number of nursing homes, assisted living facilities, and hospice centers is mushrooming throughout the country. In the years to come, you are likely to see spas for the dying, where people in their 80s, 90s, and even older, can experience regular treatments. Hospice spas will ease the pain of the dying in their last hours, days, months, and, sometimes, years. Spas for the dying may be built on a different wing within existing institutions for the aging, thus making it easier to transport residents from one section of the building to another.

# International Spa Tours in Exotic Destinations

Travel agents and spa owners will begin to offer spa packages in exotic lands. There will be a growing demand for this as more consumers want to visit spas in exotic destinations where treatments like Ayurveda, Fen Shui, and Zen meditation originated.

# Pet-Friendly Spas

Spas will become more accommodating towards pets in the future. What's more, you are likely to see pet therapy services being offered at spas. Spas will keep pace with the pet phenomenon by investing in kennels and cages. Dogs, cats, and parrots alike can seek comfort in the spa environment. Some may offer treatments for pets simultaneously as their owners receive massages.

# Mobile Humanitarian Spas

The wars, genocides, and natural disasters in all parts of the world today have brought out the good side in some people who want to travel to other countries and make a difference in a positive direction. More spa professionals will transport their skills to the needy in the developing world. Spa owners are likely to start spa education overseas for their staffs, as a way of encouraging them to engage in charitable work.

## Spa Treatments on Commercial Airlines

Commercial airlines are likely to start offering spa services as a part of their menu of services in the future. It may become possible for passengers to hire their personal masseuse during airline travel or make a treatment booking in advance as they make flight reservations. The in-flight crew may include a trained masseuse, available to give on-site massages.

# Futuristic Spas

As people become more stressed and rushed for time spas will provide virtual instant gratification for clients; the spa industry will return to its roots and go underwater to offer treatments; and the internet will revolutionize how we can experience spa treatments.

## Drive-Thru Spas

More and more people are going to be working like machines in the decades to come. They are going to want something quick to relax their hectic lifestyles. You are likely to see drive-thru spas in the future, where clients drive in for a spa treatment on the go, like in fast food on the go. For example, spa menus may include a seaweed body wrap "to go." Spas will offer stress relieving massages lasting anywhere from 5 to 20 minutes to clients in the comfort zones of their vehicles. The primary audience for these treatments will be working people who do not have the time for a complete inhouse massage.

## Underwater Spas

Deep sea exploration continues to make groundbreaking advancements, and scientists are coming up with equipment to stay underwater for longer periods of time. The idea of underwater spas takes us back to the origins of the word *spa*, that is, healing through water. Salt water contains minerals that are ideal for healing. So why not create an underwater spa? Underwater spa treatments may be linked to cruise ships, safari dive boats, and scuba diving destinations.

## Cyber Spas or E-Spas

It may be possible to seek spa treatments in cyber space. Just like the X-box enables players to become a part of the live game experience, it may become possible for guests to experience spa treatments online. Individuals can "walk through" spa treatments online, gaining relief, energy, and health through the internet without having to be physically touched by a person.

# Appendix
# Day Spa Resources

## Associations

**The American Spa Therapy Education
  and Certification Council (ASTECC)**
A nonprofit organization devoted to the academic needs of spa industry personnel. Committed to providing and nationally integrating a comprehensive graduate curriculum for those seeking a career within the industry, ASTECC encourages the advancement of spa professionals and supports the establishment of spa industry standards.
1014 North Olive Ave.
West Palm Beach, FL 33401
Phone: (800) 575-0518 or (561) 802-3855
www.asteccse.com

**American Holistic Medical Association**
An organization dedicated to transforming health care to integrate all aspects of well-being, including physical, environmental, mental, emotional, spiritual, and social health, thereby contributing to the healing of ourselves and of our planet.
Holistic Medical Association
PO Box 2016

Edmonds, WA 98020
Phone: (425) 967-0737, Fax: (425) 771-9588
www.holisticmedicine.org

### The American Massage Therapy Association® (AMTA)

A source for professional credibility, continuing education, and information resources in the massage therapy profession.
American Massage Therapy Association
500 Davis St.
Evanston, IL 60201
Phone: (877) 905-2700
www.amtamassage.org

### Associated Bodywork and Massage Professionals

For associated bodyworks and massage professionals.
28677 Buffalo Park Road
Evergreen, CO 80439
Phone: (303) 674-8478 or (800) 458-2267
www.abmp.com

### The Ayurvedic Institute

Recognized as a leading Ayurvedic school and Ayurveda health spa outside of India, it was established in 1984 to teach the traditional Ayurvedic medicine of India and to provide its ancient therapies. Ayurvedic healing includes herbs, nutrition, panchakarma cleansing, acupressure massage, yoga, Sanskrit, and jyotish (Vedic astrology).
P.O. Box 23445
Albuquerque, NM 87192
www.ayurveda.com

### Day Spa Association

Promotes members' businesses through the distribution of a membership directory to consumers and the spa industry. Provides information exchange, networking, and educational events. It protects the consumer by continuously elevating the standards of professionalism and quality in the day spa industry.
310 17th St.
Union City, NJ 07087
Phone: (201) 865-2065
www.dayspaassociation.com

### International Medical Spa Association

An association dedicated to the promotion of excellence, innovation, and cooperation within the medical spa industry.
310 17th St.
Union City, NJ 07087

Phone: (201) 865-2065, Fax: (201) 865-3961
www.medicalspaassociation.org

**International Spa Association (ISPA)**
Has become the leading trade organization for spas worldwide. It helps set the standards for, educate, and support the industry.
2365 Harrodsburg Rd., Suite A325
Lexington, KY 40504-4326
Phone: (888) 651-4772 or (859) 226-4326
www.experienceispa.com

**The Spa Association (SPAA)**
Unites and educates the spa, salon, medical, and wellness industries by offering a collaborative foundation of resources, community, and innovation for the future of the spa industry. SPAA offers educational materials, group health insurance, a quarterly newsletter, business tools, and marketing pieces.
P.O. Box 273283
Fort Collins, CO 80527
Phone: (970) 207-4293, Fax (815) 550-2862
www.thespaassociation.com, e-mail: info@thespaassociation.com

# Magazines

**American Salon**
Sales and Marketing Coordinator
757 Third Ave., 5th Fl.
New York, NY 10017
Phone: (212) 895-8446
www.americansalonmag.com

**American Spa**
Publisher
757 Third Ave., 5th Fl.
New York, NY 10017
Phone: (212) 895-8253
www.americanspamag.com

**DERMASCOPE Magazine**
2611 N. Belt Line Rd., Suite 101
Sunnyvale, TX 75182
Phone: (800) 961-3777, Fax: (972) 226-2339
www.dermascope.com

### Massage Magazine
5150 Palm Valley Rd., Suite 103
Ponte Vedra Beach, FL 32082
Phone: (800) 533-4263 or (904) 285-6020; Fax: (904) 285-9944

### Modern Salon Magazine
400 Knightsbridge Pkwy.
Lincolnshire, IL 60069
Phone: (847) 634-2600, Fax: (847) 634-4379
www.modernsalon.com or e-mail: info@vancepublishing.com

### Skin Inc.
Skin Inc. Customer Service
P.O. Box 506
Mt. Morris, IL 61054-0506
Phone: (800) 469-7445 or (815) 734-1147; Fax: (815) 734-5880
www.skininc.com

# Glossary

**Acupuncture.** The insertion of very fine surgical quality needles into specific points on the body.

**Aromatherapy.** The practice of using volatile plant oils, including essential oils, for psychological, physical, and spiritual well-being.

**Aromatic facial.** A facial with scented oil or cream that improves skin tone while reducing tension and easing away worry lines.

**Ayurveda.** A holistic system of healing that originated in India over 3,000 years ago. "Ayu" means life and "Veda" means knowledge, so the term means "the science of life." It balances spiritual, mental, and social health.

**Bergamot (Citrus bergamia).** Widely used in Italian folk medicine, Bergamot gets its name from an Italian village. The oil helps to allay depression, heal wounds, and soothe skin problems.

**Bodyscrub.** Removes dead skin, making room for new skin that is silky soft. It exfoliates, nourishes, and hydrates the skin.

**Bodywrap.** A detox treatment that rids toxins through metabolic stimulation. Algae, seaweed, and minerals are popular body wraps.

**Botox.** The trade name for *Botulim Toxin*. Botox blocks impulses from the nerve to the tiny facial muscles that are related to expression lines.

**Business plan.** Precisely defines your business, identifies your goals, and serves as your firm's resume.

**Cellulite firming.** Cellulite is a common problem among women of all ages. Spas offer cellulite firming treatments to remove the "cottage cheese" effect, especially in the buttocks.

**Chiropractor.** Chiropractors work to manipulate the spine with their hands to realign the vertebrae and relieve pressure on the nerves. Chiropractic treatment is believed to be effective for muscle spasms of the back and neck, tension headaches, and some sorts of leg pain.

**Chamomile (Chamaemelum nobile/Matricaria recutita).** Has a soothing effect and is well suited to treating children. It eases anxiety, insomnia, stress-related headaches, and premenstrual tension.

**Community foundations.** Represent the interests and resources of a large number of donors rather than one family. They limit their funding to nonprofits within a narrowly defined geographic area.

**Corporation.** A separate legal entity created through the state where the business is incorporated. A corporation has owners who purchase shares in the corporation.

**Corporate foundations.** Also known as company-sponsored foundations. They are established by corporations, but tend to operate separately by their own staff.

**Couples massage.** Two people are massaged in the same room, at the same time, by two different therapists.

**Dba (doing business as).** Refers to your legal designation once you have selected a business name and registered it with your local or state government.

**Cypress (Cupressus sempervirens).** In many cultures, the cypress tree has represented eternal life. Plato (c. 429–47 B.C.) referred to it as the symbol of immortality. Cypress oil is used to treat respiratory complaints and used in foot massages.

**Eco-spa.** A spa that makes a concerted effort to impart "green," or environmentally sound strategies to help conserve the Earth's rapidly dwindling natural resources and improve the health of the planet.

**Entrepreneur.** A leader who is able to balance the creative and practical elements and create a following to sell a product or service.

**Essential oils.** Highly concentrated aromatic extracts used for aromatherapy massage.

**Eucalyptus (Eucalyptus globules).** Traditionally, Australian Aboriginal people bound the leaves of the indigenous Eucalyptus tree to wounds to speed healing. The main constituent, Cineol, is responsible for its powerful antiseptic, antiviral, and expectorant effects. It is used in chest massage.

**Exfoliation.** Derived from the Latin word *exfoliare*, meaning to "strip of leaves;" exfoliation removes outer skin.

**Feng Shui.** The science of how human beings connect with their physical spaces. Feng Shui evolved in China through several millennia and draws from Taoism, a Chinese philosophy. The words feng shui literally mean "wind water." The practice came about as an effective way for people who lived in the mountainous regions of China to protect their dwellings from harsh winds and dangerous water.

**Frankincense (Boswellia carterii/Boswellia thurifera).** A chest massage with Frankincense can deepen breathing.

**Gentleman facial.** This facial is specific to the needs of men's skin. A thorough facial cleansing and exfoliation help to reduce shaving irritation.

**Geranium (Pelargonium graveolens).** Traditionally, geranium was used to stop bleeding, heal wounds, and ulcers. Geranium is good for acne treatments because of its antimicrobial effect.

**Grant money.** Money given for various causes. Grants are awarded to individuals and organizations for specific use.

**Hammam.** The Hammam, or steam bath, has been in existence for thousands of years and is still used today as a treatment for medical conditions or a weekly health benefit in many cultures around the world.

**Herbal bath.** Popular in Ayurveda, herbal baths use herbs, flowers, and roots to nourish the water. The nutrients in turn seep into the person.

**Herbal cosmetics.** Using pure herbs and natural substances for beauty.

**Hydrotherapy.** The use of water to maintain and restore health.

**Independent foundations.** These are also known as private foundations. They are established by individuals or families and are usually funded either through inherited wealth or wealth accumulated through a business activity.

**Indian Head Massage (Champissage).** Involves the massage of the upper back, shoulders, neck, head, and face. "Champi" in Hindi means "having your head massaged," and is the source of the word "shampoo."

**Jasmine (Jasminum grandiflorum).** Exquisitely fragranced, Jasmine is reputed to be an aphrodisiac. The flowers of the Jasmine plant, cultivated in India and North Africa, yield tiny amounts of oil.

**Juniper (Juniperus communis).** Its antiviral properties make juniper useful in treating respiratory infections and an ideal air freshener. Juniper is often used in anti-cellulite massage blends.

**Kneading.** This movement is useful on the shoulders and fleshy areas such as the hips and thighs. It stretches and relaxes tense muscles and improves circulation, bringing fresh blood and nutrients to the area.

**Knuckling.** Knuckling is commonly used on the shoulders, chest, palms of the hand, and soles of the feet for a rippling effect.

**Lavender (Lavandula angustifolia).** Lavender is an antiseptic and is used to treat acne and eczema. It is also used in herbal pillows.

**Lemongrass (Cymbopogon citrates).** Lemongrass has many pain-relieving properties. It also acts as a digestive tonic, diuretic, and antiseptic. In India it is widely used in Ayurvedic medicine to treat fevers and infections. It acts as a sedative on the central nervous system.

**Lomilomi massage.** A Hawaiian massage. "Lomi" means to rub, press, or squeeze. It may be performed with either light or deep tissue work, with rubbing, stroking, kneading, pounding, pressing, vibrating, pulling, and compression.

**Marjoram (Origanum majorana).** Marjoram was reputedly created by Aphrodite, the Greek goddess of love, as a symbol of happiness and well-being. Massages with Marjoram ease aches.

**Maternity massage.** Reduces backaches and exhaustion through the second and third trimesters of pregnancy.

**Medical spa.** The International Medical Spa Association defines a medical spa as follows: "A facility that operates under the full-time, on-site supervision of a licensed health care professional. The facility operates within the scope of practice of its staff, and offers traditional, complementary, and alternative health practices and treatments in a spa-like setting. Practitioners working within a medical spa will be governed by their appropriate licensing board, if licensure is required."

**Meditation.** The art of bringing the physical, emotional, and mental states to calmness.

**Microdermabrasion treatments.** Used in Europe for years, this treatment removes dead, flaky skin cells and stimulates the production of fresh, young skin cells and collagen.

**Music therapy.** The use of music to achieve therapeutic goals. It helps motor skills, social/interpersonal development, cognitive development, self-awareness, and spiritual enhancement.

**Need statement.** One of the elements of the grant proposal, it is the community need that the plan is addressing.

**Onsen.** The onsen is a Japanese public bathhouse (sento) with natural hot spring water.

**Operating foundations.** Private foundations that use their resources to conduct research or provide a direct service.

**Partnership.** Is formed whenever two or more people decide to enter a for-profit business venture. Typically, each partner owns a portion of the company's profits and debts, which can be set up in a written agreement between the two parties.

**Peppermint (Mentha piperita).** Grows in abundance in Morocco, where it is served as a delicious tea. Peppermint oil is also an excellent mental stimulant and digestive aid.

**Percussion.** Brisky, bouncy percussion movements are useful on fleshy, muscular areas.

**Pressures.** Deep, direct pressure is extremely useful for releasing tension in the muscles, either side of the spine, and around the shoulders.

**Reflexology.** Focuses on stimulating reflex points on the feet.

**Reiki.** In Japanese, Reiki means "Universal Life Force Energy." This energy is directly available from air, sunlight, earth, food, and water.

**Rose (Rosa centifolia/Rosa damascena).** Roses have long been associated with Venus, Roman goddess of love and beauty. Rose oil is used in facial massages and skin products.

**Sandalwood (Santalum album).** Mentioned in the *Nirkuta*, the oldest of the Hindu *Vedas* (written in the 5th century B.C.), sandalwood was used in religious ceremonies in India. It is used in Indian Ayurvedic medicine. Sandalwood is used to calm and cool the body, reduce inflammation, infection, and fever. It is popular in beauty products.

**Shiatsu.** Also known as acupressure, is a system of treating disorders by pressing firmly on the skin at precisely located points. It uses the shi (finger) atsu (pressure) to stimulate and calm the body without the use of oil.

**Shirodhara.** Used in Ayurveda, this is the pouring of a continuous stream of warm oil over the middle of the forehead to relax the body and bring peace and clarity to the mind.

**Small Business Administration (SBA).** This is a government agency set up to help small businesses succeed.

**Sole proprietorship.** The most common and easiest type of business to create. Anyone who performs any services of any kind is by default a sole proprietor, unless the business has been set up otherwise.

**Spa.** The word "spa" originates from the Latin phrase "salus per aquam" meaning "health from water." It is also the name of a small village in Belgium where the ancient Romans discovered that hot mineral springs relieved their aches and pains.

**Stone massage.** A specialty massage that uses smooth, heated stones.

**Swedish massage.** Helps to reduce tension and soothes muscles.

**Stroking.** The rhythmic flowing movements of stroking form the basis of massage.

**Tai Chi.** As practiced in the West today, it can perhaps best be thought of as a form of yoga and meditation combined. The Chinese characters for Tai Chi Chuan can be translated as the "Supreme Ultimate Force."

**Tea tree (Melaleuca alternifolia).** The Australian Aboriginal people used poultices of the leaves on wounds and cuts and smoked the leaves to clear congestion. Tea tree oil is ideal for the feet.

**Thai massage.** Manipulates the body by using unique positions for stretching and focuses on pressure points.

**Thermae.** The term "thermae" was the word the ancient Romans used for the buildings housing their public baths. Most Roman cities had at least one, if not many such buildings, which were centers of public bathing and socialization. Upper-class Romans would usually visit daily, lower-class people about once a week.

**Thalassotherapy.** A type of hydrotherapy that uses sea water as a therapeutic treatment.

**Yoga.** Derived from the Sanskrit word *yug* or "unite," yoga is the science of union that originated in India over 6,000 years ago.

# Index

Music, spa, 86–88
how to introduce, 87–88
incorporating into menu, 86
Oriental, 105
therapeutic qualities of, 87

N

Nail and hair salons, 116
Naming your business, 30–31
fictitious name statement, dba, 31
testing your spa name, 31
Natural healing, 3
Newsletter, spa, 76–77
Niche, finding your, 9–11

O

Obstacles, 26
Offline marketing, 78
Oriental
drinks, 105–106
music, 105
Oxygen infusion, 133

P

Paintings and photographs, exotic, 102–103
Partnership, 32–33
Personal savings as source of start-up funds, 19
Pet-friendly spas, 148
Philanthropic activities, 79
Plastic surgery and medical spas, 128
Postcards, marketing, 77
Practical tips for starting a spa, 37–42
Preplanning and decision-making, 14–15
Press releases, 77
Print advertising, 81
Pro bono work, 79
Property or casualty insurance, 37
Pros and cons
of being an entrepreneur, list of, 26
of starting your own spa, 14

R

Reasons for seeking spa services, 2

Referrals, cultivating, 82
Reiki healing centers, 137–138
Rejection, stoic resilience to, 43
Retreats, 138
Rice paper décor, 104–105
Rules of spa etiquette, 141–143

S

Satisfaction, 26
Sculpture, spa, 89–91
Seasonal trends, 10–11
Segments of industry, 2–3
Self-care, not extravagance, 9
Self-esteem, 26
Sensual healing, 93–99
aromatherapy, 97–99
massage, 93–97
Small Business Administration (SBA)
definition of business plan, 33
loans, 20
Sole proprietorship, 32
Spa parties as hottest industry trend, 114–116
Spiritual spas, 3, 135–143
eco-holistic spas, 136
meditation centers, 136–137
Reiki healing centers, 137–138
retreats, 138
yoga centers, 138–139
Spiritual tips for opening a spa, 42–44
Start-up financing, 17–22
Starting from scratch, planning a spa, 13–15
Stationery, spa, 82
Stress relief, 8
Success, trappings of, 43–44

T

Tamarind juice, 105–106
Tanning salons, 116–118
Teen spa, 10, 110–111
Theme, selecting a spa, 14–15